1. Family Expectations

2. Family

3. Northern Ireland genealogy

4. Women

5. The woman at the well

6. Fear

7. Anxiety

8. Jealousy

9. Anger

10. Judgement

11. Pride

12. God always finishes what He starts

13. Name change

14. Do you feel loved?

15. Death

16. God's glory in creation

17. Abortion

18. Shame

19. Failure

20. Religion

21. Whose armour are you wearing?

22. The Truth

23. Relationships

24. Blame

25. Identity

The Snowball    By Lorraine Taylor

Jerimiah 30 v 2

Thus says the Lord God of Israel, "Write in a book all the words which I have spoken to you"


Consider, if you will building a snowman, a particular favourite of mine to do. We go into the garden, and we gather a handful of snow. We crush it together, push it and shape it. It's made of the top snow, the white, pristine and perfect snow. We then start to roll it around the garden, and as we do it grows bigger. As we start to run out of snow, soil, stones and grass become stuck and embedded.

The pristine becomes discoloured with residue, it has visible and buried shrapnel, stones, mud and grass, which are so stuck that we would have to cut chunks out of it to make it pure again. We then dress it up in a hat and scarf and put it on display for all to see its faults and flaws. Its then and open for anyone to comment on it, as they walk past the garden. Even watching it melt and fall apart, into an unrecognisable puddle.

Genesis 1 V 27

So, God created man in His own image, in the image of God created He him; male and female created He them.

We were all created in the image of God. God made us like Him. We are born pure and pristine. Every child in His image. Wonderfully and fearfully made. His reflection.

When Adam and Eve sinned, they were marred. The enemy told them that they weren't complete. They weren't perfect, they lacked and if they ate of the tree they would be completed and fulfilled. They ate and sought after more than God had given them. He didn't give them as He was protecting them. They wanted to be as God, His equal or maybe more than Him?

The enemy deceived Eve and Adam went along with what she said, trying to blame her and not openly admitting his mistake. The enemy deceived but they both went along with it, both making a choice.

Each one of us is made, both male and female, in the image of our Abba Father. That's who we are, a created child and reflection of God, His glory displayed in us, even if its hidden and not obvious. We were created perfect to an exact plan and purpose; our God doesn't make mistakes. We are all unique and as individual as a fingerprint, but each one with and capable to be the image of God.

As children of earthly parents, we are told, "Oh you're the image of your mum/dad/granny etc". And maybe we look like them, but are we carbon copies of personality or individuals? Our identity was perfect at our creation. We listen to others, and we hear both good and bad and take on those comments as if that's who we are. We could be told a hundred compliments, but the one negative, bad thing, is what we cling to. We form our own identity through the lies of the enemy, the untruths and half-truths we take on as true.

We are who God tells us we are, but sometimes we listen to the one who shouts loudest or most often. The negative drowning out the positive. The discouragement being more believable than the encouragement. Some examples of our earthly parents' words may have been "Oh you did nothing but cry" "You were an absolute nightmare as a child" "You never shut up and were a pain" or maybe "You were such a good child, not like your sister she tortured me"

"Oh, you did nothing but cry" can translate in your identity to, you were annoying, a drama queen, a pain, hard work and difficult to love. This may have been an exaggeration; just an insult. Or translated by the hearer to "I am inconvenience" "I am unlovable". It may just have been a child who was frightened, ignored, lonely, wanting attention or just unsure and emotional.

Hearing "You were an absolute nightmare" could translate to the hearer in their identity to, "I am broken, a mistake"," I'll stay quiet and become quiet, be unnoticed", "I am unlikeable" "I misbehaved and made their lives a misery", it could have just been a child without company, lonely, feeling, bored left out, maybe a learning difficulty?

"You never shut up and were a pain" could translate to the hearer in their identity to, "I am too talkative", "I annoy people by talking too much", "people dislike me", "I'll stay quiet and not annoy people with my constant talking". This may have just been a normal inquisitive child, asking why and trying to learn, full of fun and enjoying life with plenty to say. It may have been a parent who was overwhelmed, busy, with too much on their mind?

"You were such a good child, not like your sister she tortured me" this could translate to the hearer as "I must not be like my sibling", "I will be compliant", "I will help all, and be good". This could mean a person who doesn't stand up for themselves for fear of causing a drama, for fear of being compared to a sibling and losing the good child badge?

These are all just suggestions and I would ask you to think about what was said to you and look at it from a different perspective if you translated it as negative. What made you shy, noisy, good or bad etc. Sometimes people don't say how they feel for fear of rejection, and other people's reactions. So, we swim with the crowd and not upstream, we go along with others and can be led astray. Like Adam, going along with what Eve said and not listening to the Lord's command.

Please don't feel I am trying to make parents go on a guilt trip, that's not what I mean at all. The enemy will take these things and through lies, half-truths and his need to steal our identity in God, he will distort and keep reminding us, whispering things and convincing us further. Presenting the evidence to back it up and sounding very convincing.

When we accept Jesus, the truth of who we are will become clear; we are to be like Him. Jesus reflects and is like His Father and we by Jesus' example with the help of the Holy Spirit are to reflect Him. To have His characteristics and to be who He says we are, the image of God. We are, if we accept Jesus, a blood washed ransomed child of God. Someone who is so loved by God that He gave His Son as a ransom, a sacrifice for our sins. Jesus took all sin upon His body for us. He gave up all for us and He endured torture so horrific we may never know or understand, just to adopt us into His family. To snatch us from the enemy and give us back our identity, who He says we are, and He is the Truth, the Way and the Life.

The hard thing to do is to let go of our own understanding of who we think we are. I hear in my work as a counsellor, "I'm afraid because I don't know who I'll be without all my hurts and regrets. My story all my things that have made me who I am, my "sticky labels" If they are saved it's easy, I just tell them "You will be like Him, the One who rolled out the heavens and who counted the stars".

Galatians 5 22-23

But the fruit of the Spirit is love, joy, peace, patience, kindness, goodness, faithfulness, gentleness, self-control; against such things there is no law.

As we start to set down our hurts and misconceptions of who we are in the flesh, we start to develop the fruit of the Spirit by the help of the Holy Spirit. We get back to who we were meant to be before we became stained and tarnished.

People describe themselves as lost but they are merely misplaced, misguided listening to others' opinions of them, to mould them into what pleases them and fits their agenda. When a person sets down all that influence from others, they can become someone who pleases God, but who they can become happy with; saying what they mean and knowing it's a true reflection of who they are.

If they are not saved, being more comfortable with their identity is still preferable to living with others' opinions of them. We usually feel we must live up to others' expectations of us. In counselling we can use the 'iceberg model' developed by Edward T. Hall in the 1970's. It tells us that an iceberg is many times bigger below the water than above. Above the water represents what people know or think they know about us. Below the water is all the hurt, negatives, experiences, shame and guilt that we keep hidden for fear of ridicule, judgement or rejection to name a few. Sometimes for the Christian this can be sin, but God sees it.

In this book, I hope to explain how we claim back our identity in Christ, by pointing out things that keep us from it. At least let you consider what has been said and influenced you and how you view yourself.

# Chapter 1    Family Expectations.

Judges 6 v 12

And the Angel of the Lord appeared unto him and said to him, The Lord is with thee, thou mighty man of valour.

At the time Gideon was hiding, threshing wheat, in the wine press. The Lord knew his potential. Gideon saw himself as from the least family in the tribe of Manasseh. And the youngest and the weakest in his family (just the type the Lord loves to display His glory in). Gideon didn't believe what the Lord told him or his identity, a mighty man of valour? He asked the Lord for a sign to prove who he was.

Gideon thought his identity was in his social standing, his place in the family, his age, his stature and his behaviour, hiding and afraid. He was hiding from the Midianites believing he was not brave or capable.

So many times, people see a lot of their identity in where they live, the money available, their parents, their siblings, age and stature etc. They, sometimes, almost start life defeated, believing that they are the least. Some people make it a goal to break the mould and they do, and can thrive and confound others, most don't. Most are a product of all that they experience and because they listen to others, how they perceive the world.

As the enemy tells them lies about who they are, they believe and sometimes become what they have internalised. If money was an issue, although a lot can still feel loved most will always feel poor and will act accordingly with the weight of the world on their shoulders; dreading becoming poor, not having enough, being hungry or poorly dressed. They will usually never feel as if they are secure and have enough. They may feed into the social poverty in their community, finding solace in others under the same burden and going along with the crowd and all that entails.

We all get told lies by the enemy, me included, from we are born. This separates us from God, the One in whose image we were created. When we ask Jesus to save us, He begins the work, along with the Holy Spirit, of chipping away at the 'sticky labels' we have gathered up.

I was born the year the 'troubles' in Northern Ireland started, 1969. The youngest of 5 children. My mum was at home and later worked as a laundress. Dad was a carpenter and a member of the 'B specials. Dad was raised a Roman Catholic and mum was a Protestant. We lived in, at the time, a neutral part of Belfast. I was a sickly child, always on antibiotics, my first teeth rotted in my gums coming out black and I had ginger hair, freckles and was tiny.

We got put out of our house by paramilitaries who didn't like our religion, as it was then. I never felt safe, mum had a bit of a breakdown and was on 'nerve' tablets and wasn't emotionally available until years later. I always felt as if I didn't belong, I didn't fit in.

Being the youngest I can relate to Gideon, I was small and skinny, the runt of the litter, once described by mums' friend as "the mistake".

When I did say how I felt I was smacked or teased, ignored and just made to feel stupid I would mould myself to fit. I felt the need to be liked, to be correct; overthinking and analysing. I based my self-worth on what others said or how they reacted to me; my ability to make others happy or like me. I didn't know my worth in Christ. Running about by the river Lagan, thrown out in the morning and if you came in again before lunch or dinner being told, "You're either in or out, come in again and you're staying in". With the result we were afraid to go in so, we got into trouble.

I loved my eldest brother; he was 19 years older than me, but I remember crying after him. My eldest sister was 11 years older than me and a teenager when I was a toddler. She was always described, mostly by herself as the prettiest one, the most photogenic. The best dressed and most elegant. My next sister the middle child, I loved and still do. We slept in the same bed and fought over the blankets, drawing a dividing line down the bed. She always won as she was older. I was close to my, next to me in age, brother, and he was always protective of me.

Mum was the disciplinarian and wasn't usually available when I needed. Mum was adopted and had a lot of her own identity issues around who she was. Mum withdrew, and still withdraws her love, when she doesn't get what she wants from you, or you don't behave as she would expect. But she was a good mum, we were fed, clean and looked after. Mum just had a lot going on in her life.

Dad loved a party in his younger days before he got saved. Dad would be drunk a lot and he loved a singsong. Even before being saved, he sang hymns. Dad used to babysit us on a Saturday and without mum knowing he took us to the pub. I learned how to pick winners at the horses and dad would nip next door to the bookies to place a bet. Leaving us with the bar staff or out playing on the beer kegs.

Dad always took time with me, telling dad jokes and watching the show jumping on telly with me. He took me swimming and to the cinema. At around 8 I realised that I had to do what mum said or she would ignore me and her and dad argued, I became a people pleaser because of this; learning to read people and atmospheres.

Romans 8 v 28

And we know that all things work together for good to them that love God, to them that are called according to his purpose.

The Lord used all my experiences for my good and His purpose. I saw the value and the worth of this ability to read people and atmospheres. Before the Lord I would try my best to keep everyone happy, changing who I was to fit in. Always feeling like an inconvenience, an outsider, not that I was, but I had forgotten my identity. I would say things and because it wasn't how I truly felt, it didn't feel genuine.

I also felt that it was pointless to dress up or try with clothes because I was always put down. I now on reflection see the insecurity of those who told me not to even try. My biggest critic based her self-worth on looks and money. I consciously tried to distance myself from being like her, in reality, we have similarities.

I became a Tomboy and got into mischief, never getting caught, small enough to hide and avoid capture. I made others laugh, so I became the one who took nothing seriously; covering all with smiles and laughter a lot of people do this being known as the funny one, but this falls apart when there is trouble; you can't fall apart and ruin the mood

Many people cover their true feelings by using smokescreens. The dyslexic child who either stays quiet in class trying not to draw attention to their self-titled 'stupidity' or else playing up and being disruptive to be removed from class; all to fit into another's 'normal'. All these behaviours and automatic negative thoughts take us further from who God says we are.

Isaiah 30 v 21

Whether you turn to the right or to the left, your ears will hear a voice behind you saying 'this is the way; walk in it'

When we are lost and can't remember who we are this is what the Lord says. He brings us back. He guides us. He sees us a perfect finished creation, just as God saw Gideon as a mighty man of valour, God sees us as the end product, perfect and a true reflection of Jesus. When He made us in His image, we were separated by sin but the Lord with the Holy Spirit perfects us and will present us to His Father someday as a reflection of Him.

When we take on others' opinions of us and cloud our true identity, we internalise these opinions, we knit them into our own self-image, and we live accordingly. Always on the defensive and never at ease, like sandpaper rubbing and eroding Gods image in us.

Psalm 139 v 14

I will praise You; for I am fearfully and wonderfully made: marvellous are thy works: and that my soul trusteth right well.

King David wrote this. He knew who he was. He was the youngest child, not even noteworthy, out tending the sheep. The least in the family. Anointed to be king but asked by his father to leave the sheep and bring food to his brothers, the soldiers. He felt righteous anger as Goliath taunted his God. Saul tried to get David to wear his armour, he didn't go himself, but wanted David to wear what he had. David knew that it wasn't him and he refused to wear it.

David knew the God he served and who it was protecting him. He went in the Lord's strength, having Him as his armour, David defeated the giant Goliath.

As we drop others armour, others' opinions and put on the strength of God we too can defeat giants, whatever form they may take. Our best armour is the identity we have in Christ. We are to reflect Him. We are to follow His example and strive to be like Him. He then directs us and guides us into our true identity in Him.

Proverbs 23 v 7

For as he thinketh in his heart, so is he

This can be looked on as Cognitive Behaviour therapy. If we think we are worthless we will act worthless, making wrong decisions. Expecting the worst, waiting to be offended and hurt, so being defensive and aggressive, or apologetic and submissive.

If we think we are worthwhile we will behave in that way. We will have confidence in our abilities in what we are and who we are. We will not accept things that aren't good for us. We will give our best and expect to receive the best from others.

The Word of God is the source of all knowledge. There is nothing new, no new thoughts to benefit others and us, all is in the Bible. An instruction manual for a better, healthier and more fulfilling way to live and to think. There is nothing new to God and therein lies the comfort. He's seen it all and knows it all, and He also knows the results and the solutions. We just have to trust in Him and ask Him to forgive and save us.

## Chapter 2    Family.

Psalm 127 v 3

Behold, children are a heritage from the Lord, the fruit of the womb a reward.

Jesus was Gods only begotten Son. He loved us so much that He gave Him as a once, for all sacrifice, a payment for our sins, so that if we believe in Him and repent, we may be saved.

Jesus was Marys firstborn son and child. Joseph was Jesus' earthly, legal father. Joseph was tasked with caring for instructing and teaching Him. Listening to the ways of the Lord. He fled to Egypt as the angel told him and returning from Egypt as the Angel told him. Joseph looked at Jesus as his own son showing no partiality.

Mark 6 v 3

Is this not carpenter, the son of Mary, the brother of James and Joses, and of Juda and Simon? Are not his sisters here with us? And they were offended at Him.

Jesus was Marys oldest son, an obedient son to His Earthly parents. But He was also God in the flesh. Eldest children are often looked on as the example for the rest of the siblings. What an example they had to follow, what a comparison! If the father dies the eldest would have been expected to be the head of the house. Caring for and providing for their mother and other siblings, helping and caring for all. Keeping the family afloat, stepping into the fathers' shoes, the head of the household.

Joseph is not mentioned later in Jesus' life, and it does not say what happened to him. Jesus had His Heavenly Fathers will and purpose to fulfil. I'm sure all would have fell on Jesus, but He knew who He was and His great responsibility, not just for His earthly family but, for all humanity and for all to come. He couldn't do what His brothers and sisters expected, who they thought He should be. Jesus knew He Had to be sacrificed, die and rise from the grave that all who would believe in Him could be forgiven all their sins and saved.

Matthew 12 v 47

Then one said to Him, "look, Your mother and Your brothers are standing outside, seeking to speak with You"

Jesus when He started His ministry had to leave His family home, He travelled preaching, teaching and healing. But He didn't listen to others' expectations of Him, who others thought He should be and what He should do. Jesus knew His identity, who He was, and He carried on determined and Kingdom minded. He did all with great love and as Jesus' mother I'm convinced that God, Jehovah Jireh, the God who provides was always there caring for her as He does for all.

This was how it used to be, but now and in my work, I hear from a lot of the youngest children that the expectation is on them a lot more as they are usually the last to leave the house. The expectations of siblings and their protests usually change how the one still at home behaves. If they stop doing and being compliant to other siblings, they are usually met with criticism and complaints.

In the law, the commandments of God given to Moses, it says we are to honour our mother and father. Jesus whilst honouring His earthly mother and father, still understood and knew His identity, He was the King of Kings, Lord of Lords. The soon to be Saviour and Redeemer of the world.

The weight of expectations and the responsibility placed on us all by others, especially family members, work colleagues, school friends and more increasingly the world and society is hard to fulfil. As we strive to do and fulfil all of everyone else's expectations of us, and then also for them to fulfil what we want of them, we can become stressed, anxious, disappointed and we would need to be superhuman.

We and they usually want all to conform to what we all want and need to make our lives better and easier. We all want others to share our opinions and be like us and have all in common, but this isn't how we are, we are all individuals.

When we take all this on board and try to please all and have them please us, not a bit of wonder most of us buckle under the weight. We may try to overachieve, running on empty, forgetting who we are, trying to be all things to all people. With Jesus, He just asks us to come to Him just as we are, He just wants us to believe and trust Him, to let Him show us to His freedom, our identity who He says we are in Him.

When we are overwhelmed, a lot just retreat, giving up under all the pressure, stopping trying. This can be where the enemy sneaks in using guilt, shame, feeling low, feeling a failure or feeling like a victim, full of resentment but afraid to change things because of the perceived backlash.

Guilt is feeling we haven't done enough, we have let others down or disappointed them by our actions or lack of. We can usually apologise or make amends, even though we are at our wits end. The Holy Spirit can convict us of sin, and we can seek forgiveness, say sorry and repent.

Shame is when we feel we are not enough. We are broken, not capable, not worthy, flawed and usually unlovable and beyond repair. This is a feeling from the enemy as it usually makes us hide from God, just as Adam and Eve hid after they had sinned, God called to them, but He already knew where they were.

When I was about eight years old my dad, who I adored, went into the next room to mine and took an overdose. Praise God that mum discovered him, and he was taken to hospital. I can still see him in a chair with a white blanket over him being taken by the ambulance men. He looked at me in guilt and I felt shame, I took it into my head that I wasn't enough. My dad didn't love me enough. This put my life into a spin. I no longer felt adored by my dad.

He no longer wanted to take me swimming, to the cinema or watch telly with me, in my mind.

At that time, I felt lonely and so sad. Mum was angry with him, and I was afraid he would try again or leave. This turned to anger in me and as I didn't want my dad to be angry with me, I internalised it and began to despise myself. The shame made me lower who I was and what I deserved from others.

This is usually the case around those left after someone ends their life voluntarily. Those left behind wonder why they didn't ask them for help. What they could have done to prevent it? Did they fail that person? Was it because they were badly behaved, just not good enough? Did that person just not love them enough to stay with them?

Those left behind are usually filled with guilt and shame, believing the lie that they could have stopped it. They had failed that person by their action's, words or the lack of. These feelings as well as the feelings of trauma can lead to anger. Anger is a secondary emotion; we all feel something before anger, be that sad, lonely, embarrassed, marginalised unfair etc.

When David was taunted by Goliath, he was angry that Goliath was insulting his God. Nothing else mattered to David and the Lord stepped in and Goliath was defeated with a slingshot and a stone. In the bible it says that Judas who betrayed Jesus was so wrecked with guilt and shame that he hanged himself.

In my work I would meet young people who have lost parents, family members or friends through suicide. They always come with the false belief that they could and should have known. They struggle so much believing they are a bad person, uncaring, selfish. They also not only feel sadness and anger but also see all their failings and flaws through the enemies' lens, telling them it was their fault.

I would always ask a client, who else was available to that person. If they had mental health issues why didn't the doctor or professionals pick it up? I ask them to look at realistic expectations of themselves. They usually at some point realise that they couldn't have changed the outcome. They are still sad but can begin to heal. They normally look at their own mortality and what happens after death?

When the person begins to realise what they may have liked to do, but what they couldn't do, they become more tolerant of themselves, kinder and more forgiving. They are also usually kinder and more concerned about others.

If experienced by young people or children, suicide can leave mistrust. They are often cautious about how they treat others, who they let close and most times they push others away. Preferring to push away rather than risk being hurt again. Abandonment and rejection all feeds into the mistrust.

Deuteronomy 31 v 8

It is the Lord who goes before you. He will be with you; He will never leave you or forsake you. Do not fear or be dismayed.

The Lord never leaves or forsakes His children, He's always there. The Lord never abandons or rejects His children. He doesn't stand waiting to punish, but rather He stands with open arms always beckoning us to come. Jesus never rejects any that call on His name for salvation. He loves all saved and unsaved. He wants that none be lost. His invitation is to all. Earthly mothers, fathers, friends, jobs etc can and do reject and abandon but Jesus knocks gently beckoning wanting to save all, He turns no one away, and wants you just as you are.

I hear people preach and post on social media about Gods punishment and His wrath portraying Him as an angry and cruel God. In reality, when you read the word, you

ee His great love and patience, unending grace and mercy. He gave us His only son to
ay for our sin!

John 3 v 16

or God so loved the world, that He gave His only begotten son, that whosoever believeth
n Him should not perish, but have everlasting life.

This is probably the best known and most quoted Bible verse. God didn't just
ove the world He SO loved the world, a treasured possession. He gave His son as a
acrifice to take all our sin. It's for the whosoever for anyone. He pardons your sins and
rings you back to be in a right relationship with Him, your creator, God.

He never abandons He rescues and holds you tight, He holds you as a butterfly,
eautiful and fragile but so gently that He doesn't crush you. He doesn't flinch at anything,
s that would damage you. He promises never to leave or forsake you.

He never rejects you, when you fall, He picks you up. He wants you to keep
ooking up to Him, to run your race. To rely on His grace and mercy, to trust in His love for
ou. If you mess up and sin, which we all do, confess it to Him, not trying to hide it He is
ust and merciful and He promises to forgive you and cleanse us.

John 1 v 9

we confess our sins, He is faithful and just to forgive us our sins, and to cleanse us from
ll unrighteousness.

He always forgives us when we ask Him, and He doesn't hold grudges. He
oesn't half forgive, taking it out of the back pocket to reprimand us. He chooses not to
emember it. If we confess and mean it; He always forgives us. Even if we haven't
onfessed yet. He doesn't withdraw or withhold His love. His love can't grow more or
hrink to less. He loves us fully no matter what and He can't love us less as it's not His
haracter. He can't change as He doesn't need to, He's already perfect. Ask Him to save
ou just as you are.

## Chapter 3    Northern Ireland genealogy

Ezekiel 18 v 20

The person who sins will die. The son will not bear the punishment for the fathers' iniquity nor will the father bear the punishment for the son's iniquity; The righteousness of the righteous will be upon himself, and the wickedness of the wicked will be upon himself.

I never heard about this Bible verse and others like it, I had always heard abou "The sins of the father being put on the son. This really frightened me not knowing what si of my own husband's colourful past might be passed on to my son, indeed my sins too!

As I investigated the Word of God more, I realised that each person is responsible for their own sin. Each person is made unique and although as they grow, the will glean both good and bad from the examples they watch. Everyone can either listen to and take on board or set it down.

In Northern Ireland with the past, we all lived through, the legacy of the 'troubles we were often persuaded by our parents and learned by their reactions and opinions. We were sometimes indoctrinated into a way of thinking, taking sides.

If you for instance, have a parent or a sibling who did wrong, maybe murder, you may live in pride of them, wanting to be like them, following in their footsteps and joining the paramilitaries. You could also feel totally ashamed and recoil and distance yourself from them living in dread of the statement "You are just like them". This statement can als be used a s a rebuke or insult "you're just like your dad"; if said in love it could also be a warning.

This identity may be so far removed from who they are, but if repeated enough they may start to believe it and believe that this is how others view them, causing shame. This can be a factor in addictions, a means of altering the mind and forgetting who others say they are. The personality whilst on drugs being different and better, or the ability to forget and dull down memories.

I've seen in counselling that as they start to realise their own identity, demystifying and looking at themselves honestly and openly, the addictions start to loose When they start to see their worth, they start to change.

When they start to realise who God says they are and their identity in Him, it's as if the scales fall from their eyes and ears. Once they realise that the past is behind, and they are a new creation in Jesus. Our future in the world is not inevitable, God gave us freewill, and we can decide what path we take.

2 Corinthians 5 v 17

Therefore, if any man be in Christ, he is a new creation: old things have passed away; behold all things are become new.

When we start our journey back to our true identity, and we read Gods Word, we realise who we really are. We are no longer a reflection of our parents and siblings we are a reflection of and being transformed into the image of Jesus.

God made us perfect, sin and others and ourselves, our own freewill changed us from who we were meant to be. The image is somewhat clouded. When we accept Jesus' invitation to believe in Him and be saved, the blood, He shed for us covers us and washes us clean from the penalty of sin. The Holy Spirit transforms us in the name of Jesus, and when God looks at us, He sees all that His son has done, not anything that we have done. Jesus, when we die on Earth presents us to His Father as a perfect reflection of Him.

In 2019/2020 a survey in Northern Ireland about personal wellbeing found across the categories; life satisfaction, worthwhile, anxiety and happiness that 45–65-year-olds scored below the average scores. When the troubles ended so many males were left with feelings of what was the point? What now? Left with guilt, shame, depression, PTSD and higher rates of suicide.

Most young men found their identity at home in their religion, listening to and watching parents. Loss of friends and family. The news, political views, following friends and the wanting to fit in. The sense of someone having your back. Also frightened men being brave in groups.

They carried out atrocities, some through hatred, bigotry, misplaced loyalty, coercion, anger, "a so-called noble cause", feelings of injustice to their people fighting over land and territory which belongs to the Lord anyhow! Some joined paramilitary organisation and then realised the intimidation and murder they took on. Having to live looking over your shoulder, all part of the cause.

An Ex-paramilitary, I won't say which group, once told me that he and another man were told to go and shoot a man. They rapped the door with their balaclavas on and the man's wife opened the door. The husband came into the hall and took a heart attack. In that instant the two remembered who they were, not murderers. They gave the man CPR, and an ambulance was called. They left before the ambulance arrived, but the man survived.

The man telling me had gotten saved and went around telling the Gospel to all who would listen. He's now in glory. He was gloriously saved, redeemed, forgiven and totally transformed into a gentle, loving patient man. The Holy Spirit transformed him into the reflection of Jesus who had saved him, his true identity, how he was always meant to be.

In addictions of drugs and alcohol bigotry isn't usually a thing. They forget about religions, as their faith in man has fallen away anyhow. Sometimes religion has been the problem that causes the addictions, in abuse and harsh treatments, hypocrisy. Religion is man-made rules trying to keep the commandments, the commandments do not require faith to keep. Faith is completely different we have faith in what we don't see. We trust in Him, and we know without doubt that our Redeemer is alive and will save us who believe and trust fully in Him.

Over the Covid-19 lockdown from 23, March 2020 so many addicts in Belfast gave their lives to the Lord. Yes, they still struggle with the addictions but most still drag the past with them. They haven't yet taken on who Jesus says they are when they come to Him.

Our legacy of the troubles tells us false truths and half-truths, the tools of the devil, about one another. Only when we look without hatred do we see. In the Lord there is no bigotry, or no partiality, all were created by God.

Acts 10 v 34-35

Opening his mouth, Peter said "I most certainly understand now that God is not one to show partiality, but in every nation the man who fears Him and does what is right is welcome to Him.

The Lord doesn't regard nationality, bigotry, borders, land or religion. All is from God, all land and people and possessions, we can't even take a breath without Him. The Lord doesn't see religion, as living by man-made traditions is not from him, it is a form of idolatry. Our God sees faith. He sees the heart. He doesn't want hearts who are hedging bets, going to church on a Sunday, claiming to be a Christian as an insurance policy, just in case. He wants a truly repentant heart, who believes and trusts in His Son Jesus, and all He has achieved for us.

Job 36 v 5

Behold, God is mighty but does not despise any; He is mighty in strength of understanding.

The Lord loves all, saved and unsaved. Even in Churches they think that their church is right and the one down the road isn't as good or Holy. The church is the people not the building, denomination or the sign above the door. The Lord wants unity in His church. The Lord sees the heart of the believer. He sees the motives of all. He knit all and understands all, He is omnipresent, everywhere at once all the time, you can't hide or deceive Him, you can try, in vain though.

Even if we confess to be saved, you can't buy your way to heaven, as some religions believe. You can't get to God because of good works or by trying to impress Him. You can't impress God because He can't love you anymore or any less than He does now. You also don't hold Him up so you can't let Him down. He is your creator.

When ex-paramilitaries get saved and step out for God some people become all self-righteous and look at them full of unforgiveness even though they themselves were forgiven. Jesus tells us in His word if you are forgiven more, you love more.

Luke 19 v 10

For the Son of man came to seek and save that which was lost.

The Lord sees the heart and soul, the motives. He knows the chain of events that has led to that point, He sees all and knows all. He knows your full story. He saw the perfect little baby beautiful and pristine being, changed and moulded and transformed, separated from God as it grows to adulthood. He knows all and understands. He still stands and offers salvation and forgiveness of sins. He loves you that much. Not one person ever in life looking with clear eyes could ever not see the Lord's hand on them, if only they look, He was always there, is and always will be, even if you don't accept Him.

Chapter 4     Women

Genesis 1 v 27

So, God created man in His image, in the image of God He created He Him: male and female created He them.

I'm not a feminist, I don't want to have to open doors for myself to lift heavy weights etc. I can if I want to, but why would I? I'm not incapable but I know that I have different skills from men. I don't think I'm better than men and I also don't believe they are better than me. We are different, we are to complement each other, not compete.

When Adam was created it was found that he had no help, so, he was put into a deep sleep and woman was formed from his rib, his side. Man was from dust and woman from Adams' flesh and bone. Like a chairman and a vice chairman, both have different roles of equal importance, each specialised in its own way but the chairman has ultimate responsibility and couldn't run anything without the vice chairman. Both have different roles and are both important.

God is a God of what look like impossibilities and contradictions. Adam the one through whom sin entered the world and the One through whom it could be removed grew from a woman, and the Spirit, a divine appointment. Mary grew and gave birth to Jesus.

Adam and Eve were naked and not ashamed or embarrassed they were just comfortable in the image of God. In no way trying to hide what God had made. As satan asked Eve "can it really be..." He put doubt in Eve's head making her doubt Gods truth. He made her discontent and deceived her; Telling her that she wasn't allowed to eat of the tree, or she would be like God. She wanted to be wise and insightful, to feel she was more.

All the enemy has as a weapon is lies and half-truths and if he can whisper in your ear and try to implant something in your mind he will. He wants to steal your identity as he knows the further, he can take you from the image of God the easier it is to manipulate and control you. The biggest fear in society now putting fear in all is, Identity theft, it's always been a blow from satan.

Eve was deceived but Adam just ate, he forgot the Lord's Word and went along with her. Throughout the Bible we see men going along with things to please women. Solomon who God had appeared to twice, set up false gods for his wives and worshipped them, even though he had met the living God, not statues. How easy men are led astray, and they always blame others for their sins. Adam just should have owned up to his sin.

2 Corinthians 6 v 18

"And I will always be a Father to you, and you will be My sons and daughters, says the Lord Almighty"

In God's eyes we are all equal. He measures all and sees all as equal. He is no regarder of persons and makes no difference in how much He loves His children, He loves us all equally. Like having two children, one who lives in the house with you and one who lives in Australia, we don't love less because a child is far from us, but it is easier to show them love when they come home and they are present.

I always thought that as female I was inferior until I read how Jesus treated women. He takes the least and He lifts them up. When He fed the 5000, the women and children weren't counted, it was more like 15,000 that were fed. They were the least, yet a woman most likely made up the food for her son to give to the Lord. He took it and multiplied the little, the bread and fish, doing one of the biggest miracles.

In counselling women don't usually know their worth, the same as most men who come to counselling. Women are made to feel that being gentle, loving and feminine is a licence for men to step all over them. Yet Jesus was gentle and loving, He never raised His voice in anger, He was compassionate and caring and He changed, transformed and made a way to redeem the whole world.

Women are being told that they must be independent and strong, they are now told they are better than men. Most don't see that they are just equal. They either buckle under the pressure from men, feeling inferior, weak and less; or they will do all they can do to belittle and run-down men trying to 'turn the tables'. In the process of exalting themselves they can damage men and themselves. If they allow man to have free reign, they can lose sight of their worth in God. We are equal, a helper, just with different skills and characteristics but all in Gods image.

The enemy uses media to make women discontent, telling them who's image they should be in. They scar and distort themselves with plastic surgery, tattoos, piercings, disfiguring themselves, so that when they look in the mirror, they may like what they see. Their image is distorted.

Ephesians 2 v 10

For we are His workmanship, created in Christ Jesus unto good works, which God hath ordained that we should walk in them.

God made us all in His image, with His nature and bodily form. Unfortunately, this image does get distorted, but we are His workmanship., He made us. The enemy tries from the moment we are born to change and distort us because in this distortion he tells us lies. He makes us feel inferior and strive after things that he tells us will make us complete.

We chase idols in our search for completeness, not realising that in Christ we are made complete. We look for money, yes, we do need it, but when we strive after it never having enough, we will never feel rich. Cars, houses, holidays, clothes, make up, beauty products, things we try to fill our need to be complete with.

Food in excess to our own needs is gluttony, but gluttony can lead to health problems and death. All things when we focus and strive for them lead to discontentment and feelings of being inferior when compared to others. Adam and Eve had all things that they ever needed yet the enemy made Eve feel discontent. The enemy whispered in her ear not his, knowing the female need to feel equal. When we realise that all things are from God and all things He can take away, we realise that it is only our mind that brings discontentment and inferior feelings. Oh, the enemy loves feelings and emotions, he can play with them and use them. Never be led by your feelings.

Matthew 6 v 33

But seek ye first the kingdom of God, and His righteousness; and all these things shall be added unto you.

I'm not for one moment suggesting that if we seek God that He will give us wealth and possessions. The Lord wants to transform you back to His image, who you were meant to be in Him. But also, the Lord clothes the lilies in the field, and He feeds and provides for the animals, and we are made in His image, and He sent His son to die for us.

When The Israelites were brought out of Egypt led by Moses who followed the Lord, they became discontent; complaining "He's brought us into the wilderness to kill us" They wanted food, He sent them the angel's bread. They needed water and it came out of a rock. They wanted meat and it rained Quail until they were knee deep in them.

God is the maker and the provider of all things. Do not fall into the trap of thinking that you provide for yourself through your own labour. Most are quick to blame God, but less hasty to thank Him.

When little girls are nurtured and loved, made to feel special. Maybe not experiencing negative comments about appearance, not being excluded or bullied feeling different. They will have more confidence, love, kindness and belief in the abilities placed in them. Living up to potential.

If not, they can shrink and hide or become haters of themselves and the world, distrusting all and trying to feel worthwhile in their ability to make others like them. They can never achieve this ever and will always feel defeated.

When we realise that our God is the creator, He made us perfect in Him. He loves us and our purpose is to please Him and be like Him. We are all His masterpiece. This allows us all both men and women to not have doubt, to overthink to second guess others' opinions. When this becomes unimportant and insignificant compared to our desire to please God we become less concerned with what others think. This gives us freedom as we aim to please God we will strive to do what pleases Him and this automatically frees us and makes us happier. But however, the enemy will still try to convince us we are not good enough.

Ephesians 6 V 17

And take the helmet of salvation, and the sword of the Spirit, which is the Word of God.

Every day we are to put on the full armour of God, available to all believers. The reason I have picked the helmet of salvation is that the helmet is as a Roman soldier's helmet. It covers the head and the ears. When it is on our heads, and we know and believe we are saved we can drown out the enemy and the whispers. We can also speak the Word of God and remind the enemy we are saved.

Jesus knew who He was in His Father, and He always quoted the Word to the enemy to chase Him. No one or nothing can stand against the Word of God. God spoke all to existence, as it tells us in Genesis.

John 1 v 1-5

In the beginning was the Word, and the Word was with God, and the Word was God Himself. He was in the beginning with God. All things were made and came into existence through Him, and without Him not even one thing was made that has come into being. In Him was life, and the life was the light of man. The light shines on in the darkness, and the darkness did not understand it or overpower it or appropriate it or absorb it.

# Chapter 5 The woman at the well.

John 4 v 7-9

Then a woman from Samaria came to draw water. Jesus said to her "Give me a drink" For His disciples had gone off into the city to buy food. The Samaritan woman asked Him, "How is it You being a Jew, ask me, a Samaritan woman, for a drink?"

Jesus had taken a detour through Samaria, and He stopped at Jacob's well, the one he had given to Joseph. It was midday and Jesus had sent His disciples into the city to buy food. Jews and Samaritans didn't like each other and were almost enemies. Also, it was a woman who had had 5 husbands and was now living with another man. Yet Jesus spoke to her and offered her living water that she would not thirst again.

The woman came to the well in the heat of the day to avoid other people. Yet Jesus knew all about her. She after talking and listening to Him ran to the city in the boldness telling all, as an evangelist "Come and see a man who told me all things that I have done, can this be the Messiah?" The disciples brought back food and she brought back people who believed because she gathered them and more believed when they heard Him. She sowed and others reaped but Jesus uses all.

I love this story of a woman so weighed down by guilt and shame, vilified, so that she carried water in the midday sun rather than face, accusers, mockers, snide comments. Yes, she had been married 5 times and now living with another. It could easily have been a man married 5 times and living with another. We often look on her and think she must have been a 'wrong sort', to put it politely, yet Jesus sought her, He uses the most unexpected to have most impact and illustrate His great love.

As a counsellor my job is to listen to the full story what leads a person to a place that they are lost and are in so much distress and pain that they seek to tell me their deepest darkest secrets. I see doing my job as an honour and a great privilege. I see men and women and children who tell me sometimes horrific stories from childhood up to now and how lost they feel.

A man's identity is usually to be brave, not to speak of their problems, to be strong, to rescue and help others, to be "the man of the house", to be a protector, not to physically hit a female. Morals and values gained from watching others, from listening to others and from their beliefs of what is and is not acceptable.

A woman, as mentioned, is usually as her lot. Some narratives about women would be she must have done something wrong, or she must be something wrong. Women are historically to be caring and gentle to do no harm and to put up with things, all good when Biblical but not when used to manipulate or abuse women, men or children.

If I was working with the Samaritan woman before she met with Jesus, I would start with her childhood, what was it like? Who was your example? Who was your biggest influence, good or bad? Who was your solid foundation, your constant?

I'd ask her how she viewed herself, her plans and ambitions. I would ask about each of her husbands and relationships. Were any abusive? Was there infidelity from her or her husbands? Were they loving and kind did she love them? What made her pick each man? Did any die? Did she get bored? Was she unable to have children? There's a saying" if you keep making the same choices you will always get the same results". I would want to know her full story.

Everyone has a story and reasons for the choices and lifestyle choices they make. If she was in an abusive relationship, her husbands would also have back stories. Each person in the bible has a back story, what got them to where they are and why the Lord picked them. I always assumed she must have cheated on them. Did she cheat, did she find it difficult to love, was there mistrust had the enemy told her or them that they or she was unlovable. As my husband says "Jesus loves us even when we can't love ourselves"

Jesus loved the Samaritan woman so much that He went out of His way to meet her. Jesus knew her full story everything and He loved her so much. Jesus sees all and knows all.

Psalm 139 v 1

O Lord, thou hast searched me, and know me.

The Lord was there at creation, He has plans for each person, He loves all equally and He shows no partiality. We don't have to hide our story He already knows it warts and all, every bit.

Jesus sees and has seen every good and bad thing we have ever done and still He loves us and gives us grace and mercy. He stands ready to welcome us and He calls us. He doesn't want religion or traditions; He wants a personal relationship with us. He sees us and examines us, He knows our every fault, failure, strength, weakness our motives.

2 Corinthians 12 v 9

And He said unto me, My grace is sufficient for thee; for My strength is made perfect in weakness. Most gladly therefore will I rather glory in my infirmities, that the power in Christ may rest upon me.

When we believe we cannot manage, when we believe we cannot be helped, transformed, saved or loved our Lord says, watch what I will do through you. Jesus loves to use the broken people as His light can shine through their imperfections and flaws.

Jesus told the Samaritan woman that He would have given her living water. The Holy Spirit is represented as living water. The Holy Spirit reflects the spotlight onto Jesus, to illuminates our means of salvation, or Him alive in us. Have you ever watched the sun hit the sea, it shimmers and shines and is beautiful. So too when we get saved and are filled with the Spirit, others can see Him in us.

The people in the city listened to the Samaritan woman they believed what she said. I can only imagine that they saw the reflection and the belief in her. Like Moses when he spoke with God the glory on his face had to be covered with a scarf. So too when we encounter Jesus. Others see the reflection of the Son dwelling in us.

Psalm 139 v 14

I will praise Thee; for I am fearfully and wonderfully made marvellous are Thy works; and that my soul knoweth right well.

The Lord made us and knows us, He has been there every step of the way. He didn't create us to abandon us. He is the good Father. He will never stop trying to bring us to Him. Even though we all have strayed from His image He will always continue to try to bring us back to Himself. He is a gentle God who gave us free will.

Jerimiah 29 v 11

"For I know the plans I have for you", declares the Lord, "plans to prosper you and not to harm you, plans to give you hope and a future".

The Samaritan woman or anyone who knew her, I would suggest, would never have imagined that Jesus in one encounter could completely transform her. He never condemned her, He loved her. He made her His evangelist. His disciples went to bring back food, she brought back people who also needed Him. She loved Him so much, she ran to bring them, she couldn't keep quiet!

This is what Jesus does, no matter what your story, no matter what your past. He knows who you are, your Identity, your potential in Him. A light bulb only works when you apply electricity and your true identity only glows when you apply Jesus.

Just as Gideon, the mighty man of valour, hiding in the winepress or David the least thought of in his family. Jesus looks past everything; He sees you and who you are and can be. He holds your future; He can grow you. He can change the direction of your life when you follow Him and trust Him. His plans for you, as it was in the beginning, is an abundant life. Jesus and His Father do not stand waiting to punish you. Like any good parent He will correct you to keep you on the correct path, but when you fall, He lifts you up. You never run out if chances with Him if you ask for forgiveness.

Deuteronomy 1 v 30

The Lord your God which goeth before you, he shall fight for you, according to all that He did for you in Egypt before your eyes.

The Lord who parted the Red Sea is the same God who fights for us. He does not and cannot change because He is perfect and doesn't need to. Every promise in the Bible, the Word of God, ifs for each of us. If He told Joshua to be strong and courageous in Him, then he tells us to be strong and courageous too.

Jesus knows all there is to know about you, even the things that you have forgotten. He knows all your intricacies, every hurt, every tear, every joy and He still loves you.

Psalm 56 v 8

You keep track of all my sorrows. You have collected all my tears in Your bottle. You have recorded each one in Your book.

He knows your pain and every tear shed. He's beside you and always has been, will you acknowledge Him? He hears your prayers all that you say to Him.

# Chapter 6     Fear

## John 4 v 18

There is now no fear in love; but perfect love casteth out fear: because fear hath torment. He that feareth is not made perfect in love.

It is difficult to perfectly and fully love someone if you live in fear. Love should feel safe, secure, mutual, trustworthy, solid, dependable, not easily ruined. It is mutual, it can conquer all and win in every situation and its free.

If there is fear, it is not perfect love. It is not from a true place and will not last. We are to love God with reverent fear, an awestruck fear of Him. If we for instance trained an animal using fear, hitting and shouting at it eventually it would turn on us. It will retaliate or won't give all that it can give.

I listen to some Christians who preach damnation to people, and whilst, if not trusting and following Christ, Hell is the other option. If someone turns to Christ in fear, is it true love? Would it help you understand how much you are loved and cared for? Or would it be a rather than the alternative, type of love?

If you realise that Jesus died purely because He loved, you and He wanted to save you. Anything done in love is better than fear.

## John 10 v 18

No man taketh it from Me, but I lay it down of Myself. I have power to lay it down, and I have power to take it again. This commandment have I received from My Father.

Jesus laid down His life freely as an atonement, a sacrifice for all to be able to be saved if they believe in Him. After enduring horrific torture and death Jesus was buried and days later, He walked from the tomb. He was seen by many for 40 days and then ascended to Heaven. When we believe and ask Him, He becomes our Heavenly Father. When we accept Him, we will want to please Him and we will repent of our sins and the Holy Spirit helps us, through all that Jesus has achieved for us.

## Proverbs 21 v 2

Every man's way seems right in his own eyes, but the Lord weighs the hearts.

We can tell people the gospel in love, always love for Jesus or along with love for others. If we love someone our motives are true and clear; we want them to realise they need salvation. We want the Kingdom to grow. When we truly love Jesus how could we not tell others about Him and His great love for us.

If we do wrong and feel loved, we will be more ready to confess our sins and tell the truth. And if we are loved, then we will be forgiven. A child loves unconditionally and if he feels unconditionally loved he will tell if he does wrong, just as us. Jesus tells us that we must come to Him like little children.

If we are unsure of the reaction, we may hesitate to come clean and confess, fearing we will be rejected, unloved and removed from those we love. If we have experienced rejection before, why would we tell and risk that happening again?

If abandoned and feeling as if we were not enough and somehow our shortcomings, contributed to this, feelings of shame, we will try to avoid feeling that way, so we hide our mistakes, our sins.

All our reactions are based on our experiences. What has happened before, what was said before, how we experienced others' reactions to us, others or themselves. This all contributes to our world view.

If only all would realise that Jesus loves us all unconditionally and never rejects, excludes, abandons, shows favouritism, is fair, is never unjust and He never quits on you even if you want to, He keeps chasing you always wanting to demonstrate how much He loves you. He has seen all; knows all and still He loves you and wants to forgive you. If w hide our sins and mistakes, they become bigger in our minds with the help of the enemy, who whispers and makes things bigger and blacker. Even if it's bad if we confess it Jesus forgives us.

If we do things in secret, we are more likely to look at and think about the what if others find out? So, we may withdraw even from God hoping He will not see, forget about us. Of course, He doesn't, He sees all and knows all. When we sin and tell Him He chooses not to remember.

Psalm 103 v 12

As far as East is from West, so far has He removed our transgressions from us.

The reason its East to West and not North to South is the North Pole. When we go North eventually, we hit the North Pole and go South again, they meet. East and West have no divider that distinguishes one from the other, it is continuous never meeting. The Lord has seen and knows every sin and He doesn't make a difference, there is no sin greater than the other as sin is sin. We can all obtain forgiveness. Never think your sin is bigger and unforgiveable all is tiny to God.

If we tell others the gospel from a perspective of fear and condemnation, are we not just being self-righteous? We are choosing to condemn and judge others. To condemn is not part of love and especially not the love of Jesus.

If Jesus doesn't condemn us, why do we condemn others? Yes, we must tell others about satan and his weapons and what happens when we die if we don't accept Jesus. But as we are told in the Word if we condemn, we will be condemned.

John 8 v 12

I am the light of the world, whoever follows Me will never walk in darkness, but will have the light of life.

Therefore, if Jesus is light and He won't be in hell then in hell it will be darkness, no light. Jesus wants to shine light into darkness, the darkest parts of our hearts to remove the things the enemy can use to steal our peace. All the things we have hidden either consciously or unconsciously. How much freer and lighter are we when we tell the truth. That's all Jesus asks, tell Him the truth, He already knows, He's waiting on you.

Genesis 3 v 9

And the Lord God called unto Adam, and said unto him, where art thou?

This was after Adam sinned, God knew where he was but wanted to give him the chance to confess. Instead, Adam tried to blame his sin on Eve. God knows all your sin in the same way He knew Adams and Eves. God didn't stand waiting to punish them, He gave them a chance, as a good Father would. He stands ready to reassure and forgive you. Yes, you may have consequences to face for your actions, but the Lord will always help you and strengthen you, when you confess and ask for forgiveness.

Each time Israel strayed from God, even after all He did for them, when they cried out to Him and returned, He defended and rescued them. Under Jesus' sacrifice, His blood, we have more protection, when God looks at us as saved, He sees all that His Son has done, not what we have done.

Sin separates us from God. We were created in His image; sin, our wrongdoings and the condemnation heaped on us by ourselves, others and the devil, clouds our image, our identity. Jesus forgiving us and saving us when we ask Him and when we repent restores us back into His likeness.

Galatians 5 v 22-23

But the fruit of the Spirit is love, joy, peace, longsuffering, gentleness, goodness, faith, meekness, temperance: against such there is no law.

When we accept Jesus, we start to return to our intended identity. Through Jesus and the Holy Spirit these are the personality traits we will begin to display. These are the things of Jesus. But love is first. His love for us, our love for Him and our love for others. If we have nothing but we have love that's enough. If we do anything, even if it works out, in our eyes wrong, if it's done in love that's enough, the Lord knows the motives of all. No matter what gifts and talents the Lord gives us, if we don't have love "it's nothing but noise".

Judas Iscariot was the apostle who betrayed Jesus; He was chosen, he was taught, he heard all that the rest had heard. He went out with the rest and healed the sick and drove out demons in Jesus' name. He was given Jesus' power and authority the same as the rest.

Judas, however, was a thief, and was with Jesus to see how he could profit from Him. He complained when Mary poured out a year's wages worth of oil on Jesus, not thinking of the poor but how much he could have skimmed of its worth.

The Lord examines the motives of each heart. He is patient and loving and will stand patiently waiting for a heart to repent. He gives us all so many opportunities, waiting for us to come to a place of repentance. He wins us over with love; Love that endured torture and death on a shameful tree, a cross, so that through His obedience and His loss, he could gain all that believe in Him.

Love is the most important thing and underpins all the rest. If we loved the Lord and each other, the world as God loves us wow what a world that would be. Would you sacrifice your child to endure horrific torture to save a murderer, an addict, a prostitute, a homosexual, a thief or a liar? Jesus died for all, we are all sinners and if He forgives us, He will forgive all. He made all and loves all, and wants none to be excluded, it's an offer to all and if we repent and change our ways with His help we will be saved.

## Chapter 7    Anxiety

Isaiah 41 v 13

For I the Lord your God keep hold of your right hand; Who says to you, 'Do not fear, I will help you'

Over the Covid pandemic and the first lockdown, we went out with Teen Challenge, Belfast. Feeding, looking after and having a great time with the homeless and the addicts in Belfast. We had a bus and stayed in the city centre from 8 – 10 p.m. I had no fear at all, of the virus, I did get vaccinated which would hint at some degree of fear.

One Saturday afternoon I was suddenly gripped by fear at the thought of going out and I considered not going. I turned on United Christian Broadcasters Radio 2 and Isaiah 41 v 13 were the first words I heard. All at once the fear left and never returned. 2 got saved that night, 1 going on to apply and start university to become a social worker.

We are told 365 times in the Bible not to be anxious or afraid. I haven't actually counted, so I am open to correction. The Lord tells us so many times to be strong and courageous for when we understand who goes before us, stays with us and holds our hand, who can stand against the Lord who split the Red Sea? The Lord can use our infirmities and fears for the best interests of others.

Roman 8 v 28

And we know that God causes all thing to work together for good for those who love God, to those who are called according to His plan and purpose.

Anxiety is a massive problem now, someone has decided to gather fear and worry and give it a title, a label that so many use. I have even young people telling me their diagnosis because mum, dad or someone else has it. I always ask is it hereditary or learned? We look to others and how they react, and cope and we can learn good and bad habits or coping mechanisms from them.

When I was younger and not yet saved going to the off sales was the most embarrassing thing! Now you can buy alcohol along with the Sunday roast, with a child in the trolley. It's become an acceptable cure for 'a bad day, or a good day or any day' Our children watch us and learn from us, they listen to and miss nothing. They see what we do, even if they don't like how it affects us, but they usually follow suit.

My mum took 'nerve tablets' or shouted. She was and is a good mum but has a big story, not for me to tell. I used to watch her and hear how she coped. I was the youngest and missed the worst of her fears. I learned to be self-sufficient and independent.

My dad, especially when saved, always spoke of the Lord, he became gentle and longsuffering and filled with joy. A true pleasure to be around. When he drank before salvation, it was different. He wasn't always there, and mum and he argued a lot.

Proverbs 12 v 25

Worry weighs a person down; and encouraging word cheers a person up.

Joshua 1 v 9

I repeat, be strong and brave! Don't be afraid and don't panic, for I, the Lord your God, am with you in all you do.

I work a lot with people who have anxiety attacks. Usually what happens is the person will be doing something that they don't have to concentrate on and boom they go into panic. Anxiety attacks can also happen from a real or perceived threat. It can be debilitating for the person.

I would think if I was in say Australia, and I was told to get into the sea from a boat, I would think Shark and wouldn't as there is a good chance of seeing one, not a big chance but a chance nonetheless that it would happen, it's an actual threat.

If I was asked to get into the sea around Ireland especially the Irish Sea, it's highly unlikely that I would be attacked by a great white, but the water is dark and murky, there would be that what if? Even if logic says no.

When in panic our heart pumps faster to get our muscles ready by pumping oxygenated blood to enable the muscles to move. Our breath becomes quicker and shallower, to get more air in. Short shallow breaths will usually make us feel dizzy, and we then think that we are going to collapse, our chest can become tight, mimicking heart attack so we panic more, releasing more adrenaline and so it goes.

Anxiety is debilitating and the causes can be quite simple and unassuming, yet they can have a huge effect. The Coronavirus caused panic to many. Anxiety about their own life, that of family members, still having to work. Watching the news and all the uncertainty.

People suddenly became aware of their own mortality and the "what happens when I die?", question. Many people in the Northern Ireland as in other parts of the world came to faith in Jesus. Many homeless gave their lives to Him. Yes, many question, but are they really saved? The Lord knows their heart and only He gives the growth. Having no home does not make you less able to be saved, it makes you less complacent and helps you see the need for a Saviour. It is each person's own responsibility to run their own race and not to look left or right.

Lots of people have left different congregations and the church has been shaken by Covid. The Lord has commanded us 365 times not to be anxious, I would hear that as a command not a suggestion. If God is telling me "Do not fear, I will help you" I'm having that.

God fought for the Israelites, He went before them, He shielded them and led them; most times they didn't have to lift a hand. They asked Him and He defended them. He delivered them from all harm. So, if that same God says to you and me, do not fear, why would you fear?

Even though God fought for them they still looked around and wanted a king like everyone else. Even though God was their King and nothing or no one could or can stand against Him.

Joshua 1 v 5

No man will be able to stand before you all the days of your life. Just as I have been with Moses, I will be with you; I will not fail or forsake you.

When Jesus is your King and you have Him, troubles will come but He is with you and will never leave you or forsake you and He will help you. He promises.

Sometimes when we worry, we don't stop the problem, we think about others' opinions, what they will say, the consequences who and what else will happen, what the rest of their life will be like. It may go from a small problem to a massive mountain. David facing Goliath but remember what happened to that bully.

When all Israel was in a panic, David knew his God and who he served. David's brother asked him why he was down at the battle and accused him of having evil intentions, just there to see the battle. David replied to him "What have I done now?" But the put down from his brother was nothing compared to the righteous anger he felt because of Goliaths taunts against God. All were panicking for different reasons. David had fought a lion and a bear whilst tending the sheep. His experiences told him that no matter how big the problem and the worry, David knew his God was bigger.

When people panic, they often have that one person who can calm them down and make them feel safe. If we all were able to understand who our God is and who fights for us, what or who would we fear? We can't and don't change anything with worry, it just makes us fight, flight or freeze. We lash out run away or are immobilized.

When the Lord shields us as He did with the Israelites and as He promises us, who or what shall we fear. If He says we are protected, then we are. If He says He guides us then He does, if He says He comforts us then that's what He does. As the Israelites stood before the Red Sea, a sea before them and the Egyptian army behind them they must have panicked. Moses told them to fear not, stand still and watch the salvation of the Lord.

Exodus 14 v 14

The Lord shall fight for you, and ye shall hold your peace.

The Lord told Moses to tell the people to go forward, against all human expectations they walked through the sea on dry land. The Lord tells us to step into all that He has for us, He tells us to come as we go towards Him, He just needs us to step toward Him.

Hebrews 13 v 8

Jesus Christ the same yesterday, and today and forever.

Our Lord never changes, he doesn't have to as He is perfect in all His ways. He is dependable, trustworthy, loving, reliable. He keeps His promises, and He never leaves us.

Anxiety can be crippling if left unchecked, it can debilitate. If the Lord tells us not to be anxious, then He already knows the outcome. He knew that He would part the sea, they just had to trust. The Lord is the answer. He knows who He is and all that He can do. He doesn't need to worry because He knows all and sees all and is all. Under the blood of His sacrifice, His blood we can trust that He has all sorted and covered, we need not worry.

Psalm 91 v 7

A thousand may fall at your side, ten thousand at your right hand, but it will not come near you.

Proverbs 29 v 25

The fear of man lays a snare, but whoever trusts in the Lord is safe.

Coronavirus was never a surprise to our God; He just turned it to good. Taking 'church' online and into car parks and fields. More were reached in new ways and innovative ways. Nothing, no one or no virus can stop the Word of God. No disaster, nothing can stop the word. If we trust in Him, He protects us. Even when we lack faith, He still is faithful to us.

Taking 'church' out of the buildings allowed many to see and hear what it was all about, breaking down walls. Church buildings are there to keep us warm and dry. When King Solomon built the temple to God, he acknowledged that no mere building could contain Him. The church are the people not the denomination or building.

Psalm 3 v 3

But you, o Lord, are a shield about me, my glory and lifter of my head.

When you ask Jesus to save you and He does just that, He is the one who gives you boldness and fearlessness. He knows your potential and what He can do through you. All you need do is hold your peace, stand still and let God be God.

## Chapter 8    Jealousy

Galatians 6 v 4

Each one should test their own actions. Then they can take pride in themselves alone, without comparing themselves to someone else.

One of the biggest causes of unhappiness is envy. When we look around at what others have, or are like, their actions or accomplishments, we can become jealous. If we are happy with who we are and content, we will not fall into the trap of the enemy.

When we know who we are, we will be more confident and complete in who we are and what we have. Each person has their own stumbling blocks, Some money, looks, houses, cars, holidays, partners, their children. So many things that we think will complete us and be the cherry on top. The 'if Only's'.

When we are lost and broken, we look at the exterior and think 'I wish I had that'. All this does is make us sad, resentful and even angry. We can become frustrated, and our focus is on gaining what we don't have. When we don't have, the enemy will tell us that we are less than others, we are substandard. Maybe he will say that others are better, harder workers maybe, all leads us to think of injustice and envy.

It's good to realise that all possessions fall away and can be lost. Looks fade and become less, then the younger are envied for their youth. Again, this causes comparison and discontentment.

Car's break, houses fall apart everything disintegrates and is ruined. A jealous heart is usually an ugly heart it is conceited, it says hurtful things to itself and others. A jealous person can say things to hurt trying to dress up as concern but usually its ulterior motive is to destroy, manipulate and ruin purely from spite.

Jealousy damages our ability to live a joyous fulfilling life. When the serpent told Eve "If you eat that you will be just like God, wiser, knowledgeable" All things she didn't want until satan told her she wasn't enough without them.

1 Samuel 7

The women sang as they played and danced saying

"Saul has slain his thousands

And David his ten thousands

Then Saul became angry, for this saying displeased him; and he said "they have ascribed to David ten thousand. Now what more can he have but the kingdom?" Saul looked at David with suspicion from that day forward.

Saul was already feeling insecure about David. He knew the Lord had left him and was with David. Out of jealousy, he saw David as a threat. The women's song only hit Saul harder because he already knew this. All his fears, worries and anxieties all became Jealousy. This Jealousy made Saul do things that he hadn't tried before. Saul tried to kill

David with a spear. He tried to have David killed but everyone loved David and they saved him, infuriating Saul more, adding to his jealousy!

1 Corinthians 13 v 4

Love is patient, love is kind it does not envy, it does not boast, it is not proud.

When we love ourselves, and others we do not envy or be jealous. We should love ourselves, not in a vain way, because we are made in Gods image, so we are worthy to be loved because of our association with Him. Love does not want what others have as we are just happy for them.

Because David knew who he was he was genuine, he was confident because he knew His God. He spoke the truth; he made good and wise decisions. David was the sort of man that the soldiers wanted to follow. They were loyal to him, they helped him and stood by him. Like the disciples who followed Jesus.

David was described by the Lord God "as a man after My own heart". David knew his identity; he didn't try to be someone else. He hadn't strayed too much from who God had made him. God's hand was upon him, He helped and guarded David. He was genuine as all trusted him, apart from Saul. He was humble, even though he had been anointed king by Samuel, he still tended the sheep. He went to deliver the sandwiches to his brothers at the battle.

David's reaction to his brothers was "What have I done now?". His brothers must have been on his case, for David to say this, he must have been blamed, berated and treated as less, as the runt.

David was anointed in front of his brothers, they all looked the part and perhaps as older felt entitled, as if it was their birth right, knowing their brother would have been king and fighting for, and alongside Saul, knowing one day they would serve their brother. They must not have respected their brother by how he reacted to them. They must have felt envious.

Then they had proved their worth, they had hidden from Goliath, if they had the same faith in their God and who they were, they could have stepped forward to fight. They were trained warriors.

When they saw their little brother step into all that God had for him and become a hero, with nothing more than a slingshot, but with the might and power of the God of Israel in him.

David was still humble and still looked after his father's herd of sheep, he still played the harp to Saul calming and soothing him. David knew how to wait on the Lord. Even though from anointing he was taunted, attacked, hunted and still he knew that the Lord's timing is perfect, he     stayed true to his character, his identity in God.

Throughout the Gospels Jesus healed, the blind, deaf, lame, diseased and dead! But the religious people were jealous; they called him the son of the devil. Complained because He healed on a sabbath. A man picked up his mat after healing, again on the sabbath. They didn't acknowledge the miracles just the traditions.

They couldn't have ever done what Jesus could, they tried to rubbish that and try to discredit and eventually kill him. A jealous heart can ruin a marriage, a friendship, any relationship it puts the owner into destruct mode, either of themselves or those around them. A jealous person is not a good person to be around and is usually better avoided.

Like a child being jealous of a sibling we can recognise it in others, but we try to justify it in ourselves. We tell ourselves that it's okay for us but it's not for others to behave in that way.

Jealous people believe they are entitled and have been overlooked. In religion people when jealous will find fault in words actions deeds or motives of another claiming Bible verses to back their theory. When shown their envy by the Holy Spirit they can choose to continue or to repent and change.

When we realise who we are when we love and accept Jesus we will know and learn our true identity. Our identity will feel comfortable, not like Saul's armour on David. Our identity will fit perfectly we will speak truth not having to worry about what we have said. We can stand on God's promises in our identity, knowing that we are indeed redeemed. When Jesus saves us He doesn't save us a little bit, it is all the way. We can confess our jealousy and ask the Lord to help us break it in Jesus' name. Jesus doesn't save you to forsake you He stays closer than a brother. Even when we are unsaved and distant from who God says we are, He is still with us, every person and anything with breath.

The Lord can break the yoke of jealousy. When we look at the blessings that we have, if we have breath, we are more blessed than the dead and if we have a roof over our head if we have food, we are warm all blessings. If we have health, we are truly blessed.

1 Timothy 6 v 4

He is Conceited and woefully ignorant. He has a morbid interest in controversial questions and disputes about words which produces envy, quarrels, verbal abuse, evil suspicions

In counselling I would see people men and women who live in not too good marriages. Jealousy is used to describe and to try and excuse their behaviours, "he/she loves me, and they don't want to lose me" The person could be living on eggshells as the other person's pride makes them think that it is OK to behave in this way.

When the other person returns the behaviour, they don't think that it's okay. They are special in some way, hurt from the past excusable and they don't deserve to be treated like this.

No person should stay in a relationship where jealousy dictates, the Lord loves us all equal, He treats us all equal and He is our example. We are to be like Him, so if we don't want treated in a particular way then we shouldn't treat or behave that way.

Jesus loves all of us and has no favourites. He knows the heart and the motives. If we ask Him to forgive us, and we change our behaviours or try earnestly, He will help us and, He will strengthen us, removing it eventually. When we realise all is from Him anyhow and He has given us eternal life what more do we need? All else is perishable only Jesus can save us.

# Chapter 9    Anger

James 1 v 19

Know this, My beloved brothers: let every person be quick to hear, slow to speak, slow to anger.

Anger is what's known as a secondary emotion; we always feel something before anger. If you see that person, or maybe it's you, and for no apparent reason they explode or implode with anger, you can be sure there is something else going on. For example, the person who was bullied and someone says something innocently or ignores or pushes them and they explode. It is probably because all those past unresolved memories come back with the trigger.

The child who was always told to stop crying as it was all they ever did! May then stop showing that emotion and will react instead with sadness which leads to anger. The person always blamed for everything, the scapegoat. That person may one day get accused of something, the injustice, the frustration, the embarrassment, the sadness may result in anger from a small or large comment. Their reaction seeming excessive to the outsider.

Anger is always perceived as a negative emotion, but it can show that something else is happening and it can allow that person to explore it, and hopefully understand and heal those hurts. There is nothing that we can feel or experience, no situation that our Lord doesn't understand or hasn't experienced beside us. Just as the Holy Spirit brings all things to remembrance so to anger can help us too if we examine its origins and reasons. Anger can also be extremely destructive.

Anger, if left, can turn into a festering wound, it causes pain it causes infection and can change a person's outlook on life. Anger is used as a defence mechanism. To show all that someone is not happy, or it can be used to push others away to leave that person isolated and alone. Feeling unloved, unworthy and full of guilt for showing their anger and hurting another's feelings even if justified. Or feeling shameful as if they are defective and not worthy to be loved.

The person faced with bereavement, feeling conflicted. Missing someone but annoyed because they took their own life or took risks and abandoned them in a way. Maybe angry at the illness, the Drs, other family members or those they feel are responsible for it. This can cause a person to implode angry at themselves for feeling this way. Feeling like a bad person.

Internalised anger is destructive it can make a person hurt themselves as well as others. Alcohol and drugs help with internalised anger. An anti-depressant drug like alcohol or cannabis can dull the front part of the brain, it slows it making memories less vibrant and easier to manage. It also makes problem solving slower, and we can make not so good decisions. Maybe the person who has been hurt as a child, they can't usually retaliate because they were a child, so they turned the hurt inwards. They ask what if I had done this? Then they grow feeling incapable, weak, not able to defend themselves with no one to express their emotions to.

So, they internalise it and start to dislike themselves. They become angry and maybe angry at the six-year-old child who never fought back! This can apply to abuse of self or watching a parent or sibling being abused, bullying, name calling etc all feelings of powerlessness.

The child with for example dyslexia, hiding in the back of class fearing being asked a question just in case they feel even more 'stupid'; so, they may stay quiet or else act out being disruptive and hopefully being removed from class.

Then they sometimes take to stimulant drugs as it gives them confidence. Hiding their self-consciousness, their doubts, their shyness. They may feel braver and more capable able to socialise. The Lord sees all our journeys every cross word ever said, every cruel action, every attack He sees all.

Psalm 56 v 8

Thou tellest my wanderings: Put Thou my tears into Thy bottle: are they not in Thy book?

The Lord sees every tear we cry, not one hits the ground that He does not see. Some people cry for joy, some sadness, some frustration, heartbreak, pain, loneliness but the Lord sees all. Anger sometimes brings tears before, during or after. The Lord still knows all that leads to that point. Anger is not an emotion that is good for us and neither are the primary emotions before it.

Psalm 37 v 8

Refrain from anger and forsake wrath! Fret not yourself; it lends only to evil.

When we have anger in us, saved or unsaved, unless it's righteous anger because of blasphemy against our God, it will lead you into sin. Sin is evil, malicious thoughts, words and looking for revenge or to hurt. Anger causes us to burn, to think constantly, avoid or hurt, to want revenge or to stop it. Even when we are angry at ourselves, we sin against God because we are saying that He made us faulty. If we continue in anger and we don't give it to the Lord whilst He is waiting to deal with it, we are missing the opportunity to allow God to be God, He can sort it when we hand it over or ask for His help.

Ephesians 2 v 10

For we are His workmanship, created in Christ Jesus onto good works, which God hath before ordained that we should walk in them.

He doesn't make mistakes. He is perfect in all His ways, and He created us in His image. So, we are made perfect. Now just because our words, actions and decision's and those of others around us have taken us away from our Saviour, doesn't mean we are faulty. It just means our identity has been blurred and changed. God gets blamed for so much. Our God is very patient and because He knows all about us and our full story He has love, mercy and grace for us.

There is no darkness in our Saviour, He is the light of the world. He is perfect as He made us perfect. We all have a purpose, He has a plan, a will for each of us if we choose to believe in Him.

Proverbs 15 v 1

A soft answer turns away wrath, but a harsh word stirs up anger.

Our Saviour doesn't stand waiting to punish us for anger, He is a good Father, gentle and loving, He speaks softly to us calling each to come home to Him. To His safety to His protection. When we do this and start to realise who we are in Him, what He has done for us, how much He loves us even though we may hate ourselves. Our hearts will soften, we can forgive because we realise what He has forgiven us.

Anger in a heart can turn a soul to wickedness and evil. The gospel of Jesus and th acceptance of it allows the Holy Spirit to change the heart, mind and attitude of all who believe in Him. Forgiveness also allows us to set aside destructive damaging thoughts. Anger can have a physical and an emotional effect. It can raise blood pressure, stress, lead to illness, disease and most of all, separate us from Christ. If we can't forgive, we ca ask the Lord and He will help us, He can give us the grace to be able to forgive. We can achieve nothing without His grace.

The Lord is our Wonderful Counsellor. To counsel someone they need to talk, they need to say what they feel, to tell their story, to look at other ways and to even be open to change. To be able to consider another way. If in my job, I get a person who just doesn't want to change but is stuck then at some point I must give up. If with the Lord, we can't give up things that aren't of God then this isn't repentance.

Anger and negative emotions need to be handed to Christ and He can change ther Sometimes we just need a different perspective, looking at it from a different angle seeing our blessings, rather than failings.

Psalm 145 v 8

The Lord is gracious and merciful, slow to anger and the binding in steadfast love.

People would often say to me about Gods anger, I would ask them to read and study the Word. The Lord led His chosen people out of captivity, He brought plagues on Egypt to release them, He split the Red Sea for them to walk across He stopped and kille their pursuers. He led them by fire at night, for heat and illumination, and by day with smoke to cover the heat of the sun, to shield them. He gave them the angels bread, wate from a stone, no one got sick or needed new shoes etc. And yet they grumbled and rebelled; this rebellion went on for hundreds of years and still when they asked, He rescued them He is an extremely loving and patient God.

No one Is beyond His reach, no one is too far gone that He can't save or rescue. No one has committed a sin that He hasn't seen before. He has seen all and knows all. As H said to Adam in the garden "where are you?" He says to you, He searches for you, and H wants to save you He just needs you to answer Him and accept His free gift of salvation

Luke 15 v 7

I tell you, in the same way there will be more joy in heaven over 1 sinner who repents then over 99 righteous people who have no need of repentance.

The Lord Jesus wants that none be lost, He wants all to be saved, to hear the gospel and to repent, and accept Him as their Saviour. The gospel is that Jesus died on the cross for our sins, He was sinless, He was buried and after three days walked from the tomb, so that any who believe in Him would be saved. Jesus didn't come to condemn the world, but to save it.

Jesus even before His crucifixion was judged. He was put on trial by the religious hypocrites. They could find no sin in Him, yet even though they knew the law, the commandments, they gave a false witness against Him as He stood silent. He went in front of Pilate, who found no fault in him, then Herod no one could find sin.

Pilate wanted to release Him. All except the religious had found Him sinless. After this judgement and after He had been kicked, punched, spat on, mocked, whipped, thorns put on His head, His beard pulled out, then they crucified Him, all mocked Him. In John 10 verse 18 Jesus tells us that He gave His life freely for us.

2 Corinthians 5 v 21

He made Christ who knew no sin to be sin on our behalf, so that in Him we would become the righteousness of God (That is, we would be made acceptable to Him and placed in a right relationship with Him by His gracious loving kindness).

Jesus took the judgement and the penalty of all sin on Himself. Judgement will come again but those who accept Jesus as Saviour are covered in His blood and will be saved from judgement because He already paid our ransom.

It's very hard to fathom that all that took us away from the image of God, our true birth right, can be restored when we accept the free gift of Jesus' grace and mercy. It's free to us but Jesus paid a heavy price that we could never imagine. He took the sin and the judgement of all on His body. He bought us salvation and healing.

Jesus doesn't condemn us He wants to save us, He doesn't send us to hell, but He must honour our choice. No one else can give us or buy, as it can't be earned, us salvation. We must accept it and accept Jesus ourselves. There is no sin that Jesus hasn't seen before.

In counselling we are to be non-judgemental. We are to see each person as an individual, unique and special in their own way. If I judge, I am being self-righteous thinking myself better; like the pharisee and the tax collector.

Luke 18 v 10 –14

Two men went up into the temple to pray, one a Pharisee and the other a tax collector. The Pharisee stood and began praying to himself "God, I thank you that I am not like the rest of men swindlers, unjust, adulterers or even like this tax collector". I fast twice a week;

I pay tithes of all that I get. But the tax collector, standing at a distance, would not raise his eyes toward heaven, and was striking his chest saying "God be merciful and gracious to me, this sinner. I tell you; this man went to his home justified rather than the other man, for everyone who exalts himself will be humbled, but he who humbles himself will be exalted.

When we exalt ourselves, we are judging ourselves as above others, if God is no regarder of persons then we are all equal before a Holy God, unworthy only for the blood of Jesus that was spilled for us, so that God sees His Sons' sacrifice and obedience not anything we do. The Lord hates a haughty look, those filled with pride in themselves.

Self-righteousness is sin in us but also it can look like condemnation to others. Most people are usually only two pay checks from homelessness. We are all very close to disaster and do not know the evil and the dangers that we are protected from. This is not of ourselves but from God's grace and mercy.

Sometimes our most cruel judge is the one in our head, who condemns us, who weighs us and finds us lacking, we carry a weight of unworthiness. Weighed down by sin. That sin that separates us from God. That sin that we try to hide from view. The shame, thinking we are not enough or the guilt thinking we haven't done enough. Sin clouds and darkens our view. it tarnishes our identity, and sin makes us fear being unmasked and facing ridicule and judgement. But if only we knew that God already knows about it. Our biggest problem is asking for forgiveness, because we must admit it, take responsibility for it, and so it may change.

In counselling a lot of people worry about leaving their faults and problems behind because they are frightened of who they will be, they fear the unknown. What would life look like? the sin is so much a part of their identity they fear the freedom. They are used to being weighed down. When a Christian asked me what they will be like without sin, and all their history, their story? I tell them it will be their testimony for what Christ has done for them by giving forgiveness, His freedom, His adoption and the privilege to be restored to His image and Jesus' ransom makes us able to come back to that.

Jesus forgives because he understands. Just as He knew the tax collector, Jesus knows the heart. John the Baptist lived in the wilderness eating locusts and honey, dressed in clothing of camel hair and a leather belt. He wasn't dressed in finery, yet Jesus said of him that there was no greater born of woman. The Lord sees the heart.

When we walk in any town or city, we will always see the homeless, hungry and broken. They are just like the rest of us all born in God's image. Their stories are usually horrific and heart breaking. These people don't need the judgement of others as they already have judged themselves. The haughty look down and the humble look up. The broken know they need help, healed and rescued but most hide from judgement.

The religious and the haughty usually judge, not themselves but those around them just as the Pharisee, listing his own attributes not recognising that all is from God. A blessing that can be removed. The Lord in His grace and mercy cares for all, and all are broken and hurt, lacking in some way. Only Jesus makes us whole.

Religious people would say that the homeless and broken, if they repent and ask Jesus to save them, can't be saved if they don't go on with the Lord. God forgive us as who are we to judge the heart of any man or woman that Jesus knows from beginning to end. Jesus tells us all to go and sin no more.

Assembly's, church buildings are fantastic for teaching and fellowship, but they are also there to keep us warm and dry. God is omnipresent He is everywhere. He doesn't look at the quality of our clothes but the quality of our hearts.

Ephesians 2 v 8-9

For it is by grace you have been saved through faith and this is not from yourselves, it is a gift of God; not by works so that no one can boast.

We can't get to heaven by good works, but we do get to heaven through faith in Jesus, trying to be good by being transformed by the Holy Spirit back into our true identity in God.

I, at the beginning struggled with this believing I hadn't done enough. I was judging myself and finding myself wanting. I couldn't get my head around the truth that Jesus can't love me anymore or any less, I am just loved. I tell others the gospel because I love Him for all that He has given me, by His sacrifice.

When we judge ourselves or others we have listened to and are listening to the enemy. He wants to deny us our true identity he wants to deceive us by telling us we are not enough. Giving us shame, guilt, jealousy, inadequacy all the weapons he has always used from the beginning. He lies, it's his nature, he tells half-truths to make it sound plausible. But the only thing he can tamper with is your mind.

If we are used to being condemned and judged, then it feels more comfortable to listen to lies than the truth, all who God says we are. We get locked in our heads, our experiences, internal, external voices. But when we believe in Jesus, He tells us who we are if we continue to listen to Him.

John 8 v 31- 32

So, Jesus said to the Jews who had believed Him, if you abide in My word, you are truly My disciples and you will know the truth, and the truth will set you free.

The word of God is the truth.

# Chapter 11    Pride

Proverbs 6 v 16 - 19

These six things doth the Lord hate: yea 7 are an abomination onto Him. a proud look, a lying tongue, and hands that shed innocent blood, a heart that deviseth wicked imaginations, feet that are swift in running to mischief. False witness that speaketh lies, and he that soweth discord among the brethren.

The first on the list is our proud look, one that overestimates them self by running others down or looking down on them. Acting as if you are superior and the rest inferior. Being proud of possessions, achievements, character, intelligence, looks, money all bring pride and sin. It's the understanding that we are all created equal, and all is from God, a gift.

I don't usually see people with pride as they usually don't realise that they need help; it makes them believe that they have arrived on their own merits. They lack nothing and they can live in the flesh assured that to everyone else they are capable, gifted to be envied in every way.

Like the rich young ruler, he asked Jesus what he needed to do to be saved. The young man kept the commandments, and with pride, told Jesus. But Jesus saw his heart, He Knew that he trusted in his great wealth. Jesus told him to sell all, give to the poor and follow Him. The young man left crying because his possessions and money were an idol, placed by him higher than God. His trust was in what he owned rather than Gods provision.

In counselling it's usually the downtrodden and the broken who seek help. When they look at those who cause them distress they can look with a degree of pride, thinking that morally they have the high ground; this may be true, but who are we to judge. To judge by human standards is to look from a viewpoint.

The devil had pride. He thought that he was greater than God and he rebelled; God cast him to the earth as lightning, along with one third of the angels who went with him. The devil thought that he was better than God and could win. If he had skipped to the back of the book, revelations, he would have seen that he's lost already!

Pride, if it was the downfall of Satan, lets us know that it is an abomination to God. All are guilty of pride at some point in our lives. Throughout our lives we have looked at others and compared ourselves. It is linked in with other emotions, jealousy, envy, greed, resentment, anger, haughtiness and judgement.

Zacchaeus was a chief tax collector, his name in Greek means innocent or pure. Zacchaeus was considered a great sinner. He was tiny but would have had a lot of power. He stole and inflated peoples' debts. All looked on him and considered him as the lowest of the low. All looked at him with pride thinking he's a bigger sinner than me.

One day Jesus was passing, the crowds lined the streets, just to catch a glimpse. Zacchaeus, because of his height couldn't see. The crowds wouldn't let him to the front. They probably tried to block his view, seeing him as beyond help and unworthy to see Jesus. Zacchaeus was so hated; the people couldn't stand him.

Jesus knew the opinion of all, He saw their proud looks, their hatred and their haughty looks. Saying at least we are not like Zacchaeus, he doesn't deserve forgiveness, he's too far gone, no one can save him or change him.

Jesus stopped and called Zacchaeus down from the tree, that he had climbed to get a better view. Jesus told him that He was going to his house for food. Zacchaeus scrambled down and all the crowd began to grumble and mutter, saying He is going to the house of a sinner. Not seeing their own sin and their own need of a saviour. There is no hierarchy of sin.

Zacchaeus, there and then, declared he would give half of all he owned to the poor, and he would pay any he cheated four times the amount. Jesus told him that salvation had come to him that day.

All Zacchaeus needed was an encounter with Jesus, that was enough. Jesus is able and can change even the most broken of people. Zacchaeus had all his wealth, food, clothes yet he knew that something was missing; he wasn't happy, or he wouldn't have sought a solution. He wouldn't have climbed a tree to be seen by others, but he did just to see Jesus. Jesus saw him, He saw his repentant heart and with joy He saved him.

Think of the witness that was. The whole of Jericho and beyond heard and saw the change in him. The power of the Holy Spirit changing him because of an encounter with his Saviour. Zacchaeus found his true identity; he a hated man was made in the image of God. The Lords' arm can touch anyone, no one is too far gone.

Luke 19 v 10

For the Son of man came to seek and save the lost.

So many believe they are beyond help, so many think that they are so broken, so filthy, so unworthy and this is a half-truth, we all are not fit, none of us, to stand before a Holy God. Because Jesus died and ransomed us, only He makes us worthy.

The religious with pride would look on others as sinners making them jump through hoops, traditions to gain salvation. This is not the gospel. Jesus' gospel is one of love. Pure unfettered love. We are all unworthy, yet Jesus cannot love anyone less than the other. We are all made equal and those who know they are not worthy are exactly the ones that Jesus searches for. He indeed came to seek and save the lost.

Never allow fear to keep you from Jesus. Fear of rebuke or rejection, that's missing the point. He loves all but He wants us to come with a humble heart recognising that salvation is a gift, not just for the well-dressed or religious or those that go to our church.

Matthew 16 v 18

And I tell you that you are Peter, and on this rock, I will build My church, and the gates of hell will not overcome it.

Jesus tells us here that He will build His church. He will build His church with the lost, the humble, the lowly. Jesus knows the heart. Just as Gideon was a mighty man of valour, hiding in the wine press, threshing wheat; So, to Jesus knows who we will be in

Him. in our true character, in His victory. Where He will take us when we believe and trust in Him and what He can do. All He asks is that we trust and believe in His ability and if He says we are all His masterpieces, then we are. We are in Gods image, when we seek Him we will find Him.

Do not let pride come between you and salvation. Do not put your trust in possessions. Do not let pride stop you from asking Jesus to save you for fear of ridicule from others. That is pride. The Roman soldiers who mocked, beat, taunted, spat on, punched, kicked, pulled out His beard, put thorns on His head, all had pride thinking He was below them. If only they had known, but then Jesus had to die to save us.

Never allow the enemy to fool you by telling you that you need more money rather than Jesus, or God's grace and mercy. Salvation is a free gift. The only thing you need to lose is self-reliance, a false self, a proud self and a haughty self, but He gives us so much more.

As a person in counselling discovers their true self as opposed to the false self the constructed personality; The one who wants to please and be accepted by all. Only problem is they will never be accepted and liked by all. If we base our worth on our ability to please others, we will live defeated and inferior.

When we realise that Jesus loves us, He accepts us just as we are. He made us right; He doesn't make mistakes; His ways are perfect. We will live to please Him to look up not around at others. We are His children, and He just wants to call us home to Him and for us to be ourselves as He intended us to be. Our true identity is in Him filled with love, joy, peace, longsuffering, gentleness, goodness, faith, meekness and temperance.

Don't mistake this for any weakness at all. Jesus was perfect He came as a lamb to the slaughter but He's coming back as a lion. No one or nothing can stand against Him. He is good, He wants us to come to Him in love and in reverent fear. Not in fear, in anger, resentment, feeling under obligation but knowing that He is a faithful, loving Father who will never leave, abandon or hate us. He will not reject us, but we need to accept Him not reject Him. We can't trust Him if we don't seek Him and know Him.

Romans 10 v 13

Everyone who calls on the name of the Lord will be saved.

This verse is repeated throughout the Bible. Jesus came to die and save the whosoever not the socially acceptable, the whosoever, anybody, anyone; no discrimination, bigotry, pride or condemnation just love, abounding everlasting unending love.

## Chapter 12    God always Finishes what He starts.

Philippians 1 v 6

I am convinced and confident of this very thing, that He who has begun a good work in you will (continue to) perfect and complete it until the day of Christ Jesus (the time of His return)

   I needed counselling when I was younger, and as part of my job I had to have personal therapy. It took 4 different counsellors. I had around 43 sessions over 4/5 years. My first counsellor asked me to become a counsellor. He planted the seed; his name was John Orr. He really helped me, and the Lord used him to start me on my journey.

   The second and third counsellors were needed as part of my training; one fell asleep in my session, snoring! The Last and forth took me through trauma counselling. Each person took me to a different level in understanding myself. Each one was useful in a different way. I am still learning and getting to know myself.

   John Orr Started the work and the rest helped me, but ultimately, I only took to each one what I felt able to talk about at that time. I had to be ready to examine issues and want to change them. The work was started and is continuing.

   Counsellors have personal therapy so that any issues they have not resolved will be looked at and recognised. This means that if similar things are brought by a client, the counsellor will not be more concerned about their own issues or be tempted to tell someone how to sort things using their own remedy.

   Counselling is done in stages, manageable chunks. Once a goal is reached an individual can go away and practise it; coming back or going to another counsellor to continue with other issues. Sometimes clients don't disclose issues or move on because they don't trust, or they may not be ready, and that's okay.

   Carl Rogers, a counsellor who pioneered the person-centred approach to counselling said, "When we know who we are, then we change". The process of change when we start usually continues. Sometimes people will revert to old and familiar ways. Sometimes change is too painful, difficult or scary.

   This is the same process when we accept Jesus as our Saviour. Jesus is the Wonderful Counsellor. He knows who we are, He guides us, and He directs us. Even the unsaved He can guide and direct. He manoeuvres people to were they need to be. Those who Know His name and seek Him He will never forsake.

   Imagine someone who knows you inside out and upside down. Who sees your full past, present and holds your future. He sees us as the finished person in Him, if only we believe and ask Him. Jesus can heal a broken heart, soothe the mind, bring about reconciliation, mend families, change outlooks; He forgives and redeems.

Isaiah 41 v 10

Fear thou not; For I am with thee: be not dismayed, for I am thy God. I will strengthen you, yes, I will help you, I will uphold you with my righteous right hand.

God tells us not to fear, not to be dismayed, because He strengthens us and helps us. Once the work begins, He helps us, He shows us. He sees all things through to completion. Our God is a wonderful God, He gave us His son Jesus and left us His Holy Spirit to guide us.

In Teen Challenge, Belfast we see a lot of suffering and struggling people; each one with a horrible story. Many pray every day to the Lord and ask to be saved. Most would say "is it genuine if they still take drugs, can they be saved?"

All I know is that when they give their life to Jesus and tears leave their eyes in repentance, the Lord has started a good work. There are all types of healings some miraculous and immediate and some a slow transformation. Mine was slow and still is.

1 John 1 v 8

If we say that we have no sin, we deceive ourselves and the truth is not in us.

We all have that, go to place, or that, go to person or thing that helps us. A lot of us don't go straight to Jesus. Many will say they do, but if you're ill do you go first to Jesus for healing or make an appointment for the doctor?

In the case of addictions, they are usually caught in a never-ending spiral of shame, guilt, negative thoughts, words, memories they can't handle, words they can't forget. Drugs can dampen the memories making them manageable. They can give confidence to the quiet shy person afraid of judgement and what others may think of them.

The Lord can indeed break addictions, but sometimes the person needs to learn how to rely fully on Jesus. It's a process, learning to trust and go to Jesus, believe in His word learning His promises and precepts. How many Christians know the word of God completely and stand on it?

If the addiction goes and there is no help or way through the intrusive feelings and thoughts that person will usually go back to the addiction. If they don't like the identity they see themselves as, and haven't yet seen who they are in Christ, where do they go? If the addiction stops them loathing themselves and makes it more manageable then it would be unwise to stop completely, immediately.

Rehab is a process; it doesn't happen overnight. It's very difficult to convince the unlovable that they are worthy and loved beyond all measure. I listen to seasoned mature Christians, believers, who struggle to see their identity. They believe that God loves all so much, but how could He possibly love them?

The devil whispers lies and half-truths into the ear, saying "the Lord won't love you you're an addict, you need to stop first". In reality, Jesus wants you just as you are. Believers may accept this most of the time but may look around as the Pharisee and the tax collector and say, "except for those people".

This pride is destructive both to our souls, and if spoken to someone else, to their souls. It can be a stumbling block of condemnation. It's our job as believers to tell the gospel. The Word of God is the power, it can transform and redeem, not us, we can't change anyone in our minds and opinions.

As in John 3 v 16 salvation it is for the whosoever. If we believe in Jesus and asked to be saved, He is just and faithful and turns none away and He finishes the work. Jesus and the Holy Spirit transform us. That's why we are tested and tried. That's why we are taught to trust through trials and tribulations. The Lord Jesus perfects us and changes us, and He transforms us back into our true identity.

Yes, we have a big part to play. We must repent and pray to our Saviour. His grace and mercy are new every day. He teaches us because He loves us. He is a good Father who even loves the wayward son.

1 Timothy 2 v 4-6

God wants everyone to be saved and to fully understand the truth. There is only one God, and there is only one way that people can reach God. That way is through Christ Jesus, who as a man gave Himself to pay for everyone to be free. This is the message that was given to us at just the right time.

Only Jesus can ransom us, only Jesus can change us, the Holy Spirit works in us bringing all things to remembrance. Only Jesus can deliver us through His blood, He ransom's us, the Holy Spirit stamps us.

Jesus wants us just as we are because just like Gideon, He knows how we will turn out, what we will become in Him. He knows our true identity. The enemy attacks as he can see the weaknesses in us. The flinches, the idols and the crutches. When we learn to trust fully, and we rest on the Saviour, we begin to understand and to believe that He has never lost a battle and He never will.

Some battles are obvious, some hidden, some we are not even aware of, but the Lord knows and sees all. Whilst we look and judge others or condemn them our Saviour tells us in His word, with the measure we use to judge others He will use to judge us.

Therefore, we look up and ahead to Him, not left or right but to Him. We are not to be as the religious, imposing our rules and laws. We are not to judge or condemn. We are to love, to love all warts and all. Just as our Saviour loves us and forgives us. The battle is His and He never loses.

## Chapter 13    Name change

Matthew 16 v 15

"But what about you?" He asked. "Who do you say I am?" Simon Peter answered "you are the Messiah, the Son of the living God"

Jesus knew exactly who He was, but He asked His disciples who they thought He was. The people had been saying all sorts of things; John the Baptist back to life, Elijah, the son of the devil, demon possessed, a blasphemer, The one to defeat the Romans and many more. He was also Joseph the carpenters son, a Nazarene, a brother and a son.

Jesus knew His Heavenly Father and His purpose. He often went away to pray on His own to spend time with His Heavenly Father, just as we are invited to do, to go to the secret place to talk to and hear from our Father.

Simon was a fisherman, a son, a brother to Andrew, a husband and perhaps a father. Simon in the Bible means 'that hears',' That obeys'. Simon was by all accounts a bit hot headed. He denied Jesus three times before His crucifixion and then he went back to being a fisherman. Jesus on His resurrection sought him out. He forgave and restored him. Jesus renamed Simon, Peter meaning 'the rock', 'stone'. Jesus gave him a new identity.

Matthew 16 v 18

And I say also onto thee, that thou art Peter, and upon this rock I will build My church; and the gates of hell shall not prevail against it.

Jesus gave Peter a whole new purpose and identity, along with a new name. The Lord knew that Peter would deny Him, but He also knew the plan and the purpose He had for him. The Lord doesn't regard sticky labels that others attach; He knows our identity in Him.

Jacob was a twin who took his brother Esau's' birthright, even so Esau gave it up. Jacob means 'supplanter' interpreted as one who seizes or usurps. God changed his name to Israel which means in Hebrew 'God contended, wrestles with'. Another interpretation means 'triumphant with God'. God renamed Jacob because He knew His will for his life with Him. so many more are renamed in the Bible.

I see a lot of people with different diagnosis, they for the most, see the label as a badge, a sticky label that defines them; It becomes their identity. For example, a badge of dyslexia, most of the time, from my experience says to the person that they are maybe 'stupid or incapable'. In America 10% off the population are dyslexic, yet 35% of company founders are dyslexic. Yet a child will feel shame, usually they will hide in class to avoid answering questions or they will be disruptive to be put, hopefully, out of class. There are always exceptions, and some do not let any badge define them.

The broad spectrum of learning difficulties can't change how a person perceives themselves. Parents may say for example, "This is our Steven/ Stephanie and they are or have ADHD". The diagnosis usually being bigger than the individual under it.

Kids with ADHD are usually seen as disruptive, hard work, all over the place. They are sually just quicker, easily bored. nicknamed 'Ferrari brain' rather than the rest of us. who etermines if they are wrong, or we are? My God doesn't make mistakes.

We can change our identity according to your sticky label, being an image of who thers say or the diagnosis says. Albert Einstein said, "everybody is a genius, but if you idge a fish by its ability to climb a tree, it will live its whole life believing that it is stupid".

We were all made with gifts and talents, the Lord giving each creation as He knew est. Sometimes, indeed with God, He uses what we consider our greatest fault to stound the wise, to astound us. God doesn't make mistakes. When we see our true otential through the hands of the creator, we can see ourselves, as not broken but as nique. Unique as a fingerprint, all designed to fit together with no one made to be xcluded and left out. We can all learn from each other.

When we believe the labels that others, or we, place on ourselves, to define us we an be estranged from our true identity and our God-given purpose. The devil wants us to oncentrate on our perceived flaws, he will whisper that we are broken and of no use. He ill try to shame us into hiding away; retreating from others where he can then corrupt who e are.

Many addicts have so-called learning difficulties they find solace in addictions, they an take on the identity that the drug gives them. Filling them with confidence with, for xample, cocaine. Calming them down with cannabis. ADHD medicines dull down ppetites and some people take cannabis for the 'munchies', in affect self-medicating. /hen the head is filled with traumas, hurts, heartache's, loss, low self-esteem and they nd a drug that can alter these things and may make them more manageable the lost and uffering may turn to drugs and alcohol.

There are many addictions that serve the same purpose as drugs and alcohol. For xample, shoplifting; especially if the shoplifter is angry or hurt and they want to hurt omeone else, maybe a spouse. The person who is hurting and feeling as if they are roken being addicted to the buzz of gambling. The sex addict. The shopping addict. The od addict. All hurting people with their own needs and addictions creating an idol or a lse god, from whom they believe they are helped. When in reality, it causes them so uch hurt and harm.

These addictions or idols will also harm those around them. The effect being death, uicide, losing possessions, children being put in care (the future hurting generation), ivorce, family breakups. The guilt of not enabling an addiction for someone, and the hame of the addict or their family members who live in it.

Therefore, we are to have no false gods, because off the damage it can cause, the lse hope of help or of a cure to our problems.

John 5 v 21

tle children, keep yourselves from idols.

Corinthians 10 v 14

herefore, My beloved, flee from idolatry.

Anything that would stop you from relying on God and trusting fully on His Son Jesus, is an idol. The Lord calls us His beloved. He knows what is best for us what is destructive and can destroy us. Stopping us from enjoying life and being free from our need to feed an addiction.

When we worship Him, we no longer need false idols or gods. Through the sacrifice of Jesus on the cross and our acceptance of His free gift of internal life and forgiveness of our sins when we repent, He fills us with all that gives us life. We are built up and strengthened, protected and best of all we are transformed into the image of our Saviour. All were created in the image of God, but when Adam and Eve took of the tree and they felt the shame of being naked, the devil whispered lies and half-truths in their ear. The devil can only hurt the mind.

Genesis 3 v 11

God said "who told you that you were naked? Have you eaten from the tree of which I commanded you not to eat?"

We were not made for shame; we were not made to feel we were not enough. The enemy told them they weren't complete and gave them, if only? and then told them they should be ashamed.

When we realise who God made us to be and we realise that He loves us no matter what we are, or what we have done. We can live in freedom. Allowing Him to define us and to transform us into His image. We don't need false useless gods when we serve the true God.

Following and worshipping the true God allows us to realise that He didn't create us to harm us. The Lord made us to enjoy us and live in His creation, a beautiful world, unfortunately being corrupted. Our Lord knows who others say you are, He knows the things others say you can't do. He knows your flaws and all your weaknesses. But the Lord knows your heart, your potential and your strengths He knows what holds you, restrains and confines you. The Lord loves to show us His power and glory by using our weaknesses and flaws.

1 John 4 v 4

Ye are of God, little children, and have overcame them; because greater is He that is in you, than he that is in the world.

When you realise who made you, who asks you to repent and believe in Him, you will realise who comes to dwell in you when you accept him. He doesn't just visit you but comes to dwell, live in you. Jesus has never lost a battle and He never will. The same Spirit that raised Jesus from the tomb could potentially dwell in you if only you would take His free gift.

He doesn't want you without the labels, the addictions He want you just as you are here and now, imperfect and broken. All your broken pieces in His hands can be fixed and made beautiful. Do not make the mistake of thinking that you need to stop this or change that first. Repent, believe and ask Him. He is all-powerful and He wants to change you and transform you. Will you allow Him?

It is better to look up in humility at the cross of Jesus than to think you are sorted and look down at others or yourself. Accept Him and allow Him to change you and save you. He already knows you and He loves you, warts and all. He can't love you anymore than He already does.

# Chapter 14   Do you feel loved?

proverbs 3 v 12

For whom the Lord loves he reproves, even as a father corrects the son in whom he delights.

In a loving household there must be boundaries, limits to what is perceived as acceptable. These boundaries and limits are what make all as children, and adults, feel safe and loved. If they are fair and just, we know that, although we may not like them, they are designed to keep us safe and to let us know that we are loved.

As parents, correction should not be simply to put down and to make our children angry. It should be administered from a place of love and genuine care; To ensure our children stay on a good path, to minimise risk, to keep them from getting into unnecessary trouble. Although as children we would love to do our own thing it will ultimately end in no direction, or misdirection.

A parent is there to love us, help us grow, help us to develop to be able to live to our full potential. They feed us, they clothe us, they nurture, they protect, they keep us warm, housed, have fun with us and help us in troubles; nurturing us to the best of their abilities.

Ephesians 6 v 4

Fathers do not provoke your children to anger but bring them up in the discipline and instruction of the Lord.

Children are very clever; they may not be academically clever, but they can perceive if you are genuine, if you mean them harm or just even your mood. If they come into the house and there has been an argument, they can tell by the atmosphere, facial expressions, tone of voice, over exuberance that is used to show that nothing is wrong.

Children can read a room, ready to run away ready to intervene if a parent or a sibling is being hit or shouted at. Children are very brave. A child who is abused can read what's going to happen again. Some children will take being hit or abused to save a sibling or getting involved to deflect it from a parent.

I often wonder how a child reasons with all this in their head? I see a lot of adults diagnosed with depression because they either didn't intervene or were too young to be able to. Also being unable to protect themselves. Even the older one for example who stands up to dad and is say, being put out of the house for trying to do the correct thing.

The loving environment is not always there. The ideal is not always realistic. Even in so-called Christian homes where the veneer would say a loving home, at home in reality, could be like a battlefield; lovely on the outside but horrible on the inside.

John 12 v 43

For they loved the glory that comes from man more than the glory that comes from God.

People who play at, who put on a show for others and hide behind religion forget or don't care that the Lord sees all, and He knows all, He sees the motives and intentions of each heart. The Lord doesn't require religion He requires faith. When parents hide behind religion and try to justify their actions by blaming the word, He sees, and He knows.

Many young people become anti God through the treatment they received from so-called believing parents. They then think that God hates them; that He is bad, waiting with a stick to rebuke and discipline them. A dictator and not a loving creator. I hear questions like "how could God do this to me or allow it to happen?"

This so called 'vengeful' God gave His sinless, perfect Son to die for us, so that through Him we could be saved and set free. Everyone has a testimony, a story to tell even if we are not saved, we can see the Lord's hand on our lives. It's usually put down to luck or fate when in reality it is a loving Father trying to protect His creations.

When I was younger if my parents tried to tell me to do something I often rebelled and did the opposite. I usually realised that I should have listened, but I rarely admitted that I was wrong. We are all rebellious in nature especially as we move further from our true identity in God.

The Lord knows who we are, He knows we think we know best. He sees us trying to find our own solutions, trying to fix things in our own abilities and strengths. Sometimes we do OK, most times we get a temporary fix a plaster over a wound. In patience the Lord waits for us to ask him to fix things.

Revelations 3 v 20

Behold, I stand at the door and knock. If anyone should hear My voice and open the door, I will come in and dine with him, and he with Me.

This promise is not that of a vengeful God. The Lord knocks gently asking quietly for us to let Him in, so that He may instruct us, He may guide us, and help us. the Lord wants to sit with you, He wants to eat with you and you with Him. He wants to spend time with you.

The Lord loves you and He loves all equally. He knows we are all rebellious and He waits patiently until you realise that you can't do this on your own. You haven't the strength on your own. He wants to give you rest, to love you as a good parent, the good Father. He loves you even when you rebel, He doesn't abandon or disown you. He will never leave you even if you reject Him, He will just honour your decision.

I work with family members of addicted parents. I know sometimes it's parents of addicts also. Children of addicts believe that they are unlovable, not enough to stop a parent from drinking or abusing drugs. Sometimes these 'damaged' young people will repeat the cycle by becoming addicts or addicted parents. Some will be anti-drugs and anti-alcohol. But most nearly all will suffer mental health problems or depression at some point. The young man who sees dad hitting mum or mum hitting dad who believes that's what marriage is like.

The young woman who thinks that an abusive relationship is all she deserves. All this leads to a breakdown of the family. What is meant to be the place where they feel safest becomes a place where they feel unloved and a place of deep shame. They can't or won't tell friends and will hide or else do the same behaviours.

An addicted parent can't easily put in place loving boundaries and limits. A child without these boundaries usually coming to counselling as a teenager or adult says "if my parents had bothered to put in boundaries, I wouldn't be like this. My life would have been different".

John 13 v 15

I have set you an example that you should do as I have done for you.

Jesus is our example; we are to do as He did and be as He was. If we were all instructed in the ways of the Lord and not only us but those around us, all we encounter, all being examples of Him we would all recognise our need for Him. We wouldn't have all the problems or the issues that we have. We would love each other far and above anything else. Our parents would teach us and instruct us from love, having received the same themselves.

Luke 15 v 18-20

I will set out and go back to my father and say to him: father, I have sinned against heaven and against you. I am no longer worthy to be called your son; make me like one of your hired servants. So, he got up and went to his father. But while he was still a long way off, his father saw him and was filled with compassion for him; he ran to his son, threw his arms around him and kissed him.

This is what the Lord does when we stop living rebellious lives. When we realise that we are broken, we can't do it on our own and we need help. The Lord is always there just waiting for the heart that seeks Him. The heart that knows it has sinned. A heart that no longer wants to rebel. Our Lord Jesus runs to us and welcomes us male and female, He runs to us and hugs and kisses us.

Luke 15 v 7

I say onto you, that likewise joy shall be in heaven over one sinner that repenteth, more than over 90 and nine just persons, which need no repentance.

When we stop fighting and rebelling, realising how much the Lord loves us and we turn to Him, the angels in heaven rejoice. We all need saving. We all need to know unfailing true love. There is nothing that we have done that would ever stop the Lord from loving us. He doesn't want to punish us; He wants to welcome us home as His little children. He wants to help us, instruct us and guide us. He wants to let us know and show us who we are in Him.

1 Peter 2 v 9

But ye are a chosen generation, a royal priesthood, a holy nation, a peculiar people; that ye should show forth the praises of Him who has called you out of darkness into His marvellous light.

The Lord calls us all to rebel, to rebel against the world in all its wickedness. To be peculiar, odd for following His ways, a member of His family beloved and much loved.

# Chapter 15   Death

John 11 v 33-35

When Jesus saw her sobbing, and the Jews had come with her also sobbing, He was deeply moved in spirit (to the point of anger at the sorrow caused by death) And was troubled and said, "where have you laid him"? They said Lord "come and see" Jesus wept.

Jesus had delayed going to heal Lazarus, He could have healed him without going near him. Jesus had gone to him knowing that He was going to raise him from the dead. He was going to raise him, for the glory of God and for all to see the miraculous and for them to believe and follow Him, Jesus.

Jesus didn't cry because Lazarus was dead, He cried because of the pain and distress caused by death. Death was not meant to be. The enemy brought death when he went into the garden of Eden. Death causes people to hate and blame God. The unbelievers and some believers say, "if God exists why does He allow this to happen?"

'Jesus wept' is the shortest verse in the Bible but it shows the heart of God. It shows how He hates death, it shows His Love and compassion for us. It tells us what upsets our Lord and Saviour. Jesus gave up His life for us, He put on death and then He walked out of the grave alive, never to die again.

Romans 6 v 23

For the wages of sin is death, but the gift of God is eternal life in Christ Jesus our Lord.

When we stray from being made in God's image, being marred by sin, we must pay penalty. This was because of Adam's sin. God is a Holy God a loving Father, but He must be the same, He can't change how He judges or that would be injustice, unfair. All hate unfairness, being treated unfairly or differently. God must treat all as equal and judge all. Therefore, God gave us His sinless Son So that He could take on the penalty of all sin, today yesterday and forever. He took all of God's judgement, He was judged, He remained silent. He was mocked, beaten, spat on, punched, kicked, ridiculed, accused, whipped and crucified. He took ALL sin. He has seen all sin and knows all sin Even though He Himself never sinned.

All the sin we try to hide, the sin we think that no one could ever forgive, Jesus knows about all of it. He's already paid for it. If He hadn't paid for it already, He would have to be sacrificed again and again each time someone sins.

This forgiveness and our repentance mean our debt is paid. Jesus paid for your sins and mine. Once we ask Him, and with a truly sorry heart then He forgives us. We are washed clean by His blood, then when our Holy God looks at us, He sees all that His sinless Son has done.

This then makes us part of His Church, not a building or a denomination or a religion. But Jesus welcomes us into a relationship with Him, we are sealed by the Holy Spirit stamping us as under the blood of Jesus. Saved, redeemed and washed.

Acts 2 v 21

And everyone who calls on the name of the Lord will be saved.

We cannot be saved because we are 'worthy', we are 'good', we are 'nice' we 'behave' ourselves, we have 'no faults', we 'did well at school', we 'have a good job', we 'don't smoke', we 'don't drink', we 'don't take drugs', we 'don't swear', or we are 'good living'.

Not one person can stand in front of God worthy. We are all sinners, we are all stained, dirty, filthy in front of a Holy God. Only because Jesus saves us and covers us in His Blood can we come before our God.

Ephesians 2 v 8-9

For by grace are ye saved through faith; and that not of yourselves: it is the gift of God. Not of works lest any man should boast.

Imagine being in court in front of a judge, having been caught stealing. 10 witnesses saw you and you were arrested. Your solicitor tells you that you are going to jail But you go in front of the judge, and you tell him you are sorry, you confess all and ask him to forgive you. The judge then says, 'okay away you go and don't do it again, take this letter of recommendation from me to say that you will not be judged or condemned by witnesses again in front of me'.

You would be surprised to say the least, overjoyed maybe or just relieved. Now I realise that God sees what you have done, all of it. Nothing hidden and still He says I want to forgive you and I want to save you. No one can condemn or accuse you in front of Me again.

Mercy is not getting what you deserve; grace is receiving better and more than you deserve. The Lord wants none to die. He wants to save all.

Philippians 1 v 21

For to me, to live is Christ (He is my source of joy, my reason to live) and to die is gain (For I will be with Him in eternity).

When we are saved and understand and believe we are saved and we realise that when we die on the Earth, we are alive forever in Eternity, we can understand what Jesus has done for us. We can't go to heaven unless we accept Jesus. A mass after death can't save us, because we were nice or help the sick, homeless or orphans, this cant save us, only Jesus can save us.

Only a truly repentant heart that trusts and relies on the grace and mercy of God through the blood and the name of Jesus can be saved. The Lord doesn't want to send you to hell, but He will have to honour your choice. If you accept Him and rely on Him knowing that all that is past is forgiven you, then you will begin to be transformed into His image, back to your true identity, the image of God.

When we are forgiven and we know that our sins are gone, the Lord chooses not to remember them. We are asked not to remember them also. The bit that some struggle with is forgiving others. But if we look at our great amounts of sin that He chooses not to remember, then we must forgive others their sins against us.

When we don't forgive, we can still be filled with hurts, anger, resentment thoughts of revenge; this is sin. The Lord works on all hearts and forgives all sin we can leave it with

Jesus, give Him the burden to carry, knowing we are safe and secure in our salvation through His forgiveness and redemption. Sin is sin no matter how big or small we perceive it to be. All sin takes us away from God. Even not praying is sin.

1 Samuel 12 v 23

Moreover, as for me, far be it from me that I should sin against the Lord by ceasing to pray for you: I will instruct you in the good and right way.

Samuel didn't agree with the sin of Israel; what they were doing but he understood that he had to pray for them. To intercede for them, so that they would come to their senses and repent.

We are to pray for those that sin against us. not for our own ambitions, wanting others to change to treat us better, but rather that they change and realise that they too need Jesus. We need grace to be able to forgive fully, but God gives us this if we ask.

The Lord sees all and knows all. He sees the motives of each heart, and he sees true repentance.

Many will say to me if they hear of people being saved, but is it a true salvation and repentance? God forbid that I would ever think that I could judge the heart and motives of another, just in case the Lord judges me!

As believers we are to tell the gospel, the good news of Jesus. He died for our sins on the cross. He died was buried and rose again alive, so that whosoever calls on His name shall be saved. It doesn't say may be saved it says shall be saved. It is not my job to save. It's not my job to judge. The Lord gives the growth, the Holy Spirit moves; He is the great comforter, counsellor, He changes us, He guides us, He Keeps bringing us back to Jesus. The Holy Spirit reflects what Jesus has done for us.

The Holy Spirit changes us back to our true identity in the image of God, a loving Father. Through Jesus' sacrifice we are reconciled to our Heavenly Father.

Ephesians 4 v 32

And be ye kind one to another, tender hearted, forgiving one another even as God for Christ's sake has forgiven you.

The more we have been forgiven the easier it is to forgive. The broken and wayward are quicker to forgive in their brokenness. But we are all broken, and we all need Jesus.

## Chapter 16    Gods glory in creation

Job 12 v 7-10

But ask the animals, and they will teach you, or the birds in the sky, and they will tell you; Or speak to the earth, and it will teach you, or let the fish in the sea inform you. Which of all these does not know that the hand of the Lord has done this? In His hand is the life of every creature and the breath of all mankind.

A lot of people do not believe in God, as followers of Christ Jesus know Him. They have their own belief of who God is to fit their minds. Have you ever heard, there are many gods in different forms? A higher power to fit man's own beliefs. Or there is no God? But all believe in hell; all believe in the devil.

Even followers and believers of Jesus struggle with who God is fully, we can never ever know and never will as He is beyond comprehension. Many believe in science, but science only proves the power and majesty of God's creation. Look at humans. All made in God's image yet each unique and individual. Even identical twins differ in their nature. People talk about 'Mother Nature' ignoring the fact that God is nature. He made all and He is in all.

Jeremiah 23 v 24

Can a man hide himself in hiding places. So, I do not see him? Declares the Lord do I not fill the heavens and the earth? Declares the Lord.

The Lord has filled the heavens and the earth. The beauty of our world created by God. The very colour of the sky which changes and is beautiful. The majesty of the mountains, the power of the roaring seas, the force of the winds, and the feel of a gentle breeze. the planets suspended in the heavens, the stars, the intricacy of all creation. The so-called eco system; everything has its place and its purpose. If one part or one animal is extinct there is a consequence.

If we lose the bumble bees and insects crops will fail. They pollinate plants by the hairs on their legs. Tiny wings able to carry them in the air over vast distances. Every creature and every person wonderfully and fearfully made. How could all this be from a so-called Big Bang or explosion.

Numbers 14 v 21

But indeed, as I live, all the earth will be filled with the glory of the Lord.

The glory of the Lord is in plain sight look around you. Nothing can change His power and His majesty. The Lord does not and never has made a mistake, what looks like chaos and chance to us, has been intricately planned and made each part working together. The glory of the Lord is visible to all.

Habakkuk 2 v 14

For as the waters fill the sea, the earth will be filled with an awareness of the glory of the Lord.

We can't deny the glory of the Lord, if we look, truly look and see. Even in science it confirms that all is complicated and works perfectly; all with a purpose.  Before the foundations of the earth, the Lord had a plan and purpose for us all and knew exactly what He needed us to do. He knows why He made us and our part in the world. We are all important each one in his or her own uniqueness. All perfectly made by God.

When the Lord made each thing, He placed us perfectly, He knows our full potential. Not one thing ever made or ever to be made is a mistake. When we sin and leave God's perfect plan for us our God already knows. He knows what lies ahead for each person. He always waits patiently with perfect timing. We may not see it, but He knows.

Consider the person who can't find their car keys and is running 10 minutes late; they find them only to pass an accident that had happened only 10 minutes before. We can't and don't know what the Lord protects us from. He wants us all to accept Him. He has left us so much evidence to show us who He is. Where is the evidence for hell? Yet all believe it exists. We can't say it, yet we can see the heavens, we can see creation, but we are blinded by the enemy who tells lies to keep us from Jesus and salvation.

The devil can only tell lies and half-truths designed to deceive us and keep us from the truth. If we are deceived into thinking that all came from an explosion, in all its destruction, all the pain and devastation an explosion brings; we will live in chaos, thinking all is random and all is fate. there will be no hope, no truth or no gratitude.

John 8 v 32

Then you will know the truth, and the truth will set you free.

Over lock down in COVID many people became despondent without hope, as the media and the devil peddled fear. They became aware of death and the frailty of life. They were removed from friends and families; told not to touch or get too close, to stay isolated away from each other. Afraid to visit unable to visit in case they spread the virus to their loved ones.

Many people lived in isolation and the mental health problems that this caused. If they said to me about death, I asked them what they believed happened when we die? Most said nothing, you just are in nothing. Some however said they hoped that heaven was real and that they would be with relatives and friends already dead. They wanted hope.

A lot of people think that if you die, if you are a nice person, you will go over a so-called 'rainbow bridge'. These people want there to be a heaven, but they don't want to accept Jesus to be able to get there and have made-up or have believed someone else's lie. The truth of the gospel is being watered down, diluted, almost changed to make it pleasing so as not to annoy or upset anyone. As it says in the world, we are not to tickle the ears of people, we are to tell them the truth and the truth will set them free.

We cannot change the word of God. We cannot alter it to fit our own agenda. Dismissing parts because it may mean we will need to change. Choosing to bend it to fit what society tells us. The enemy is peddling half truths about the Word. He will tell us a bit of truth but change its intention and true meaning and he will use anyone he can to spread it.

The Lord's truth is that He loves the whosoever, it's not an exclusive select people. He loves us all and wants that we are all saved. But His word tells us how we are to live,

59

we as believers do not hate unbelievers, or we shouldn't because the Lord is the only judge.

The gospel is that God loved us SO much that He gave us His perfect Son as a ransom, a way to escape death. It's through His obedience and His death on a cross. When we believe in Him, repent and ask Him, He saves us, no exceptions, but if we truly love Him, we must try very hard to keep His word.

If the Lord tells us to turn from sin in all its forms and we decide we don't like that part, then we are saying that God is wrong. We must all seek the Lord and His ways and pray to Him. We must talk to Him, to seek Him and rely on and trust in Him.

James 1 v 5

If you need wisdom, ask our generous God, and He will give it to you. He will not rebuke you for asking.

If we want to know or understand our God, we can ask Him. I'm not an intellectual person I'm not well educated; if I don't understand I will ask the Lord to help me, and He always does. My God, your God wants you to know Him. He wants you to trust fully in Him. He wants you to learn His ways and His promises. If you seek Him, He will always be found. Even the unsaved, the atheist will accept prayer or pray when they are in trouble. All have an understanding in some way of our God and their need for salvation.

The so-called stiff necked or stubborn may not want to lose face by calling on the name of the Lord, but eternity is a very long time. I have spoken to so-called terrorists who pray because they know about God, but they fail to realise about repentance. With our God even a mustard seed of faith is enough to move a mountain. How much can a powerful and loving God do with a mustard seed of faith in each of us? We as believers are told to confess sin to Jesus and repent each day so as not to give the enemy our foothold.

The Lord can change and transform any heart. He hears the prayers and loves to welcome all the repentant. God seeks us all out and draws us unto His Son. He chooses us and that is why we should never ever ignore His call. His grace and His mercy are a free gift.

Ezekiel 34 v 11

For thus says the Lord God, behold, I Myself will search for My sheep and seek them out.

The Lord searches for His sheep. He alone will build His Church. The Church is His worldwide believers, not a denomination. We are all important in the body of His Church as on the Earth, if one thing is missing it has an effect. The Lord wants us to have one purpose in unity. To love Jesus to follow Him and to tell of His gospel so that as many as possible can be saved. So that none will be lost.

We are to tell them from love, not hatred not condemnation but from hearts filled with joy, just wanting to share the good news that Jesus is the truth. He never lies, He speaks truth, He keeps His promises, and He loves beyond measure. That is the truth. He is the only way to heaven. Through Him His love and shedding of His blood.

# Chapter 17    Abortion

Psalm 147 v 3

He heals the broken hearted and binds up their wounds.

The Lord sees our tears. He collects them in a bottle, and they are written in a book. Not one tear comes from the eyes that the Lord doesn't see. As a baby in the womb, we have so much potential. And every one of us was once a baby. We all started the same a small couple of cells ignited, miraculous in and on off itself.

Our Lord has plans for each and every little baby. Even Jesus came into the world as a baby. Yes, He was the Son of God, but He was also fully human too. The whole worlds salvation and redemption rested on a tiny little baby. King Herod tried to kill Him, he slaughtered all the little boys of age two and under. In Egypt the first-born boys were ordered to die, and Moses was rescued, as a baby, by 2 midwifes, his mother and sister; the man who would lead the Israelites from captivity and through the Red Sea.

These little babies surviving a death sentence, all growing into great men and women. If abortion had been available what would our world look like now? So many children made in the image of God the creator, by the creator; killed and destroyed not even taking their first gasp of air. Those little children of course go straight to the Lord, but has earth missed out on what could have been?

Maybe among those dead was the person who would have found the cure to cancer or dementia or another breakthrough. Our God has designed all things and all humans as a perfect system by where He allows us to discover cures, and innovative technology. Do not be fooled into thinking anything is of man. Our God provides absolutely every single thing that there is or ever will be and that we need.

The enemy whispers in the ear of the pregnant woman "You can't even look after yourself", "You are too young", "You're an embarrassment", "You will be rejected and disowned", so many lies the enemy tells. Mary was thought to have been a young teenager when she had Jesus. She was engaged to Joseph.

If the Lord has blessed us with a baby, who are we to lift our hand against it. Many women and young girls feel pressured into abortion, being convinced that their life will be ruined or encumbered by a baby. Some use abortion as contraception.

Some women are told that they must get rid of a baby because the alternative is so bad. An abusive partner, who is physically, emotionally or sexually abusive can make a pregnant woman fear for the safety of a baby, preferring the alternative. The lie being told that they can't leave. Where would they go who would want them? They are convinced sometimes that they are useless, unlovable, hated, good for nothing and lucky to have any attention whether good or bad.

These women don't realise that the Lord is bigger and more capable than anyone or anything. In the Lords will for a child anything is possible. The sad thing is that when a baby is aborted that is only the beginning of the story. Women are usually secretive about having an abortion; wrecked with guilt and shame.

Just like Adam and Eve hiding from God in the shame. Shame tells us that we are not enough, we are a substandard human being. The enemy will fill them with the condemnation, the feelings of emptiness, the what ifs; what have I done? What would that child have been? When eventually the abusive relationship ends, the feelings of loneliness, and the having nothing left can be overwhelming. Shame is a lie from the pit of hell. The only thing the enemy has to attack us is our mind, our thoughts and fears.

Guilt makes us aware, or feel that we have done wrong, we have murdered or killed. The only thing is that usually if we do wrong, we can apologise or make amends. We can't bring back the little lost life. That little gift that we rejected.

I don't want to make women feel worse but rather let them know that even though you feel like the world's worst ever sinner, He can still forgive you and He still loves you.

Jerimiah 1 v 5

Before I formed you in the womb, I knew you. Before you were born, I set you apart.

Before the Lord formed you in your mother's womb, He knew you. He knew the plan and purposes He had for you. He knew and knows every child, every little baby it's toes and fingers all special and all perfect. The Lord doesn't make us to disown us. He made us in His own image and if He made us, He would not reject us, or not forgive and keep us.

Matthew 18 v 10

Beware that you don't look down on any of these little ones. For I tell you that in heaven their angels are always in the presence of My Heavenly Father.

All children, all babies are special to our God and Saviour. He knows each one and forgets none. He made us all wonderfully and perfectly. Each one of us equal, each one of us special to Him, He Shows no partiality.

Our God is the good Father, the one who loves us and wants the best for us. He knows what's going on in your head. He sees behind the closed door; He sees your tears. He sees the fear the enemy has placed in you. He knows your circumstances, but He also adores you and your baby. Each creation that He makes has an angel in His presence, looking after and protecting.

Psalm 139 v 13

You made all the delicate, inner parts of my body and knit me together in my mother's womb.

We are all the Lord's work. The Lord loves us all and He Gives the gift of a baby. What is harder, a woman not able to have a baby, or a woman who disregards a baby?

What of the father of an aborted baby? All their hopes and dreams in a child. The law of man would say that they have no say. It's the woman's right, it's her body. Men, and young men left devastated but because of the world they can't voice their opinion. Their son or daughter disregarded, killed and that's okay? If they speak out, they are taking away the woman's human rights. If they complain they are sexist. It's not their body. These men can't speak of their anger to any great degree. They can't voice an opinion as it falls on deaf ears.

Usually, these emotions and feelings are internalised they look at the should haves and could haves and as the baby can't come back, they can't speak about the mother, and usually end up hating themselves for their perceived failings. These men are trapped feeling they should have stepped in, stopped it and yet they didn't and couldn't.

Not only women suffer after abortion but also men, grandparent's, friends. So much hope and potential is in this little human and someone has the right to kill it, because of the lies of the enemy?

Psalm 127 v 3

Children are a gift from the Lord. They are our reward from Him.

All children are a gift from God. But if we throw away or destroy a gift, how can we see the joy and the love before we even open it. We decide even before we look at it, that it's going to cause us more damage rather than adding to our lives. Each child made in God's image is a little blank canvas. It is the Lord's. All our bodies were made by God, they are not off us. We cannot will, even a hair to grow.

The same Lord at work in creation, is the same Lord who has blessed you with a little child. We place so many hopes and dreams on children, wishing their lives away. Then they grow to the stage that they leave home. They have their own children and grandchildren.

If we truly know who we are in Christ, His image, to please Him and be like Him. We understand that we are to follow Him and be like Him, we realise that our children are there to be nurtured and loved. Even if before we knew Jesus, we tried to please others to be someone or something we are not. If we realise that we are perfect in Him and each baby can be the same, we will embrace and play our part by teaching our children about Him.

Do not listen to the enemy when he says there is no other way to have a life. A life in the world is centred on the self and what we can get for ourselves. We can choose, we are self-centred, self-obsessed, we have self-esteem. All is internal, all about us, and external, what others think of us.

When we accept Jesus as our Saviour and He gives us our identity in Him, we no longer must strive to be something we are not. We no longer must pretend, He knows us. We become more concerned about pleasing Him. We reflect who He is, a perfect reflection. The world may hit you and ridicule you but when you know who you are, your identity, it doesn't matter what others have said, or if they avoid you or what they think of you.

It's all about who Jesus says you are, and He says you are special, unique and loved. If you raise a child, He will always help you, even if you don't believe in Him, He is always there. If you leave an abusive relationship, He will help you. He can mend the broken heart and mind.

God never ever breaks a promise. His promises are the Bible verses, His word. He is the truth, and His word is true, it will never change. It is a powerful life changing word. it is a living word that applies to each and every person who reads and believes it.

# Chapter 18    Shame?

1 Peter 2 v 6

For in scripture, it says see, I lay a stone in Zion, a chosen a precious cornerstone, and the one who trusts in Him will never be put to shame.

Shame is an emotion that we were never made to bear, the enemy brought shame into the garden and placed it on Adam and Eve. Shame says we are not enough, this in itself is a sin, as we are in God's image, He made us. Shame made Adam and Eve see their nakedness after they had eaten of the forbidden tree. The enemy told them that they were not good enough missing of knowledge, not complete. They needed the knowledge to fulfil them. They knew they had done wrong, and this led to guilt for their wrongdoing. They tried to hide from God.

Shame and guilt are used by the devil to try to contaminate and destroy us all. We all at some stage experience shame and guilt. Shame however leads to so much more; it is destructive and leads to self-condemnation. All of us as human beings will try to hide shame.

The devil called into question Eve's intellect, asking her "really did God say that you would die, don't be daft. Of course, you won't die but God knows that your eyes will be opened, and you will be like him, knowing the difference between good and evil. Now maybe Eve wanted to be equal to God. Or maybe she wanted to please God and not be evil? But in the garden the only evil was satan, and Eve maybe couldn't distinguish the difference, it was all new to her; Just as a child cannot at a young age distinguish evil when satan dresses it up as good.

A paedophile will tell a child that it's normal, this is what happens. It's OK, it's allowed, it's what everyone does. They will try to normalise this evil behaviour. A paedophile is demonic; satan robbing a child taking their innocence with lies. Just as Eve was deceived with lies and lured to sin. So too a child groomed. A child used to doing as adults tell them. "Be a good boy/girl and do as you're told"? There is also the vulnerable child who craves attention, love and affection. Who sees gifts and money as proof of caring. Lured into evil. Then when something happens, they are immediately told "you can't tell anyone" And the shame hits.

They will be told things like, "if you tell no one will believe you", till the child hides it and withdraws, becoming quiet. "If you tell they will take you away", fear is brought in making the shame bigger, as if they tell they will lose their family, and their family will disown them. Adam and Eve hid from God, as what if He found out would He hate them?

Another lie told is "if you tell I will kill your family", this is scare tactic of satan that brings, not only shame but, huge responsibility, way beyond what a child could or should have to endure. A child or a young person or even an adult may always feel that they must hide this secret. The child in shame is made to feel as if it is all their fault, they did it, they encouraged it, they allowed it. All lies of the enemy all made to condemn and destroy a young innocent life.

A young boy raped and torn by maybe even the physical feelings, did they like the feelings? Then they must be homosexual, the confusion that this causes. The man must have picked them because they must have known they were gay? The shame sometimes makes these boys believe they can't be with a woman, thinking no I'm gay. I am not suggesting that this is what makes men "become" gay. I meet a lot of gay men who say that they have been abused as children, causing confusion. Not every gay man has the same experience.

The young girl who has been abused who feels dirty, ashamed and when they find out that it's not "normal", they will usually hide it for fear of what others will think and say. The young girl who can't bear to be touched who can't enjoy a relationship as the fear and trauma are too great. Never really able to live a life of marriage and kids. Always thinking that this is what she is good for, not realising that what happened was wrong until she is older and hears of other experiences.

Both men and women abuse; family members, family friends, people in positions of authority, strangers all types of people. Satan uses many tactics, but all bring shame. All tell us that we are dirty, not worthy, unlovable, disgusting, second rate, broken, damaged and irreparable.; All the people that God loves to use and glorify His name through. When we believe we are born in the image of God you can see the difference, He calls us His masterpiece, not a mistake but a work of art.

A lot of men, who I would talk to, say that if they were raped by a woman maybe as an older child or a teenager although society would joke about it and say maybe "well done son!" God forgive society. The men say they grow hating women, they try to regain control, they may become domineering, abusive to wives, partners. The hurt, and the pain can be transferred to others all from the one incident.

Someone, I don't know who, said if the devil can hit one nail 100 times it will do more harm than 100 nails once. If one incident can wreck and ruin a lot of lives, then as far as the enemy is concerned it's a job well done. It's a never-ending cycle. The child, of a child now an adult, who's been abused, could either be extremely loved and protected or abused. The same with a woman who can't stand contact from her husband and may become unavailable to her child. Feeling such shame that they are incapable to love.

Sometimes a girl (but sometimes boys too), will believe that all she is good for is to be mistreated and abused. The cycle of wrong choices, or rape, domestic violence and a repeating of the pattern is hard to break. All a result of the enemy hitting that one nail.

Satan always uses the same tactics, lies and half-truths. He uses lies to say we should be ashamed, even giving us so-called evidence to back it up. It can play in the mind on a loop, repeating and condemning. No wonder drugs, alcohol and other addictions happen and offer relief. They can't handle all the memories, and addictions can fade the feelings of shame. Hiding and not letting others know how dirty and broken they are, masked by addictions.

John 10 v 10

The thief comes only to steal and kill and destroy; I have come that they may have life and have it to the full.

From the very beginning in the garden of Eden we see the tactics of the enemy, saying to Adam and Eve that they are stupid if they think they will die. Then the shame kicks in and they hide away after they have been lured into sin.

When a person, who has been abused, tells of the abuse it helps. It allows the secret, the foothold off the enemy to be broken, his lies to be exposed. Hidden lies and secrets can do so much damage to the mind. Not only does it mess with the mind, if they have shame also who do they tell?

Most partners would struggle to understand why certain things trigger a reaction, or an explosion, or an implosion in their other half. When they realise the reasoning behind such reactions, they are helped to understand and can, perhaps, help with that persons healing process now that they realise why. Many abused people if they can't live with the shame, will self-harm, form addictions, self-sabotage etc.

John 16 v 32

I have said these things to you, that in Me you may have peace. In the world you will have tribulation. But take heart; I have overcome the world.

Abuse of any kind is demonic; it is not off God. There is no darkness in God and be assured that God sees all, and He knows all. Jesus overcame the world He loves you and He wants to heal you. He is a good Father. He is the opposite of all that is evil. The devil lies, Jesus is the truth He can't lie.

Galatians 4 v 7

So, you are no longer a slave, but Gods child; and since you are His child God has made you also an heir.

When you trust in and believe in Jesus you become Gods child, an heir to all that He has for you. He takes away that shame when you realise who He says you are, and He forgives you and welcomes you. You are His creation. He loves you so much that His son died for you, not to condemn you but to tell you that you are beautiful to Him. You are special and you are loved by Him. He saw and continues to see all your hurts and everything that has brought you to this point in time.

Jesus is a gentleman, He does not force you to come to Him, He calls you gently. He wants nothing from you, He just wants to let you know that He loves you with all your flaws. He sees the broken as His little children and He wants to rescue you and save you if you will let Him.

Isaiah 43 v 4

Because you are precious in My eyes, and honoured and I love you, I give men in return for you, peoples in exchange for your life.

We are all precious in God's eyes. He made us all and created us in His image. The enemy tries so hard to steal us, to shame us, and to devastate and wreck lives through all that he does.

The Lord wants to save you. The Lord wants to protect you. He wants to guard and to shield you. He wants to welcome you with love. He wants to forgive you and to love you.

ll those consequences of your hurt, those behaviours hidden in shame, the foothold of he devil; the Lord wants to change them and transform them to give you peace and joy.

The Lord ultimately wants to free you. He wants to break the bondage of hurts. He wants to repair your broken heart, your broken body He wants you to live a life knowing hat you are loved beyond all measure, far beyond anything you could ever imagine.

ong of Solomon 4 v 7

ou are altogether beautiful, My darling; there is no flaw in you.

This is how our God sees us all, how He sees you He wants to minister to you. He wants you to know that in Him, in His identity, the person He knows you are, you have no aws. When you are covered, with Jesus' blood you are perfect. You are not dirty, filthy, nlovable to Him, you are precious, and He just loves you.

He wants you to ask Him to save you and He turns none away. To acknowledge lim as the Son of God and ask Him. "Lord save me" is a prayer and He listens for you to ay it and He will keep His promise and save you.

## Chapter 19    Failure

Matthew 14 v 27-31

Jesus immediately said to them "Take courage it is I don't be afraid". "Lord if it's you" Peter replied, "tell me to come to you on the water". "Come" He said. Then Peter got down out of the boat, walked on the water and came toward Jesus. But when he saw the wind, he was afraid and, beginning to sink, cried out, "Lord, save me!" Immediately Jesus reached out His hand and caught him "you of little faith" He said, "why did you doubt?"

Probably, Jesus' walking on the water is one of the best-known stories of the Bible. was always taught about Peter lacking in faith and how he should have trusted in Jesus, and he wouldn't have begun to sink.

All the disciples were petrified. They had just witnessed Jesus feeding 5000 plus women and children from 5 loaves and two fish. They had lifted 12 large baskets of broke pieces each and had the evidence off the miracle beside them, but still they were afraid.

Although frightened Peter still got out of the boat. He trusted Jesus enough to step into a storm. Then he looked at the storm and began to sink. He didn't scream and lose sight of Jesus but cried out to Him "Lord, save me!". A perfect prayer, called from great need. He didn't try to clutch for the boat, he didn't try to swim, he just called out to Jesus his saviour. An example to us all. Knowing who could and would rescue him.

Jesus lifted him up and asked him why he had doubted. Jesus just reached out His hand. Peter didn't walk on the water by faith in himself, he didn't in his own strength, it was Jesus' power and authority. Peter then walked back to the boat with Jesus. Peter got out of the boat and tried. He, in Jesus, achieved something miraculous. Imagine having that story to tell your mates and family, putting that on social media!

As for the other disciples, they stayed in the boat clinging to a piece of wood, looking on as Peter came back to the boat, did they say, "my turn". They could tell the story about Peter walking on the water, but it is not as good as doing it yourself, but what a thing to see. Some cling to Jesus some cling to a boat. But when we cling to Jesus and wood of His cross then the storms will subside if we focus on His ability and not our own.

I meet a lot of people full of regret, feeling that they have wasted their lives. Usually because their identity is one of not being capable, being stupid, not able, foolish. Also, the are afraid of feeling ridiculed or being laughed at. And yes, these things may be true or may happen, but Jesus was mocked, condemned, judged, ridiculed and yet He kept going He was obedient to death, He knew the outcome. The victory He would win for us.

Don't be like the other disciples, in respect of, don't let fear of failure stop you. Don't look at other people doing the things or, living the life you would like. You will live up to or down to who you listen to. You can live by your own limits or to the Lords endless and infinite ability.

1 John 4 v 4

Ye are of God, little children, and have overcome them: because greater is He that is in you, than he that is in the world.

It's very uncomfortable under the weight of other people's opinions of you. Their expectations that they didn't achieve but put onto you and then they criticise you as being a failure if you don't achieve them. But usually, other people's expectations are not what you want.

Remember when you were small and you had a goal, an idea of what you wanted to be when you grew up. Everyone asked you and you said the same thing until you were told "lower your expectations", "you'll never achieve that", "you'd be better doing this or that". Then you would dread the question and start to answer either, "I'm not too sure" or you would change your goal.

I wanted to be a stunt woman; I don't know why but I just wanted to be. I set myself up for so much criticism, so I changed my answer, the Lord said "let's do exploits, take risks" so I'm now achieving more in Him.

Expectations don't stop, the questions of, have you not got a boyfriend or girlfriend? Are you not married yet? And on the wedding day are you going to have a baby? Which then leads to, no baby yet?

So many people put others under pressure. Constantly asking us what we have achieved, what we have done and what we are going to do. When we pair this all with a lack of confidence, self-doubt in our abilities and our capabilities; trying to achieve something that's not what we feel comfortable with or want to do we will feel all sorts of pressure from others and from ourselves.

Judgement can come in many forms and ways. We judge ourselves based on comparison to others' achievements. We judge ourselves by our inner voice, the inner critic. The inner voice of criticism and condemnation from other people telling us and pushing us. Trying to push us down the road that they wanted to go or failed on.

Judgement comes again and shame for past failures. I always say we don't learn when we achieve, we learn from failures. We learn what not to do, we learn from fear of judgement. But it's what we do with the teaching. Do we stay in the boat and watch, or do we step out onto the water and keep trying. Failing means at least we have tried.

Some people stay in the boat by citing their own excuse. Sometimes it's easier and more comfortable than trying and achieving. Some people feel so at ease with the familiar feeling of failure That they just don't try. The teenager who doesn't take an exam because they believe they will fail, but that's better than turning up full of hope and failing it. They don't even imagine that they could pass.

People hide behind their age saying that they used to do this and that, but now they are too old. Abraham was 100 when Isaac was born. The Lord tells us to run our race to the end not to stop and sit down, but to get over the line. Some people will hide behind an illness or an infirmity. The woman who touched the hem of Jesus garment probably had to crawl on the ground through the crowd full of determination. Bartimaeus was blind and when discouraged and told to shut up he became more determined and called Jesus louder.

Philippians 4 v 13

I can do all things through Christ who strengthens me.

Our God gives us our very breath and has gifted each of us in some way. Without Jesus we can achieve some things and will probably pat ourselves on the back. If we don't achieve, we will maybe experience shame and guilt, reinforcing our own and others negative beliefs of us. When we accept Jesus as our Saviour and we trust fully in Him and rely on Him in full repentance, the miraculous happens. We can walk on water; we can do the things in His ability in His strength. When we realise that we may not be capable in our own opinion of who we and others say we are, but that when we realise who Jesus says we are in His Image just like Him, we can rely on and rest in what He can do through us.

If we stop striving in our own agenda but what He wants to achieve through us, our life will have a purpose, His purpose. Our life will have momentum, our life will be filled with achievements for Him. Others will look at us and not see us but see the reflection of Jesus in us. When we stand in a storm and we cry out to Him, He is always there, He will always take your hand and help you, He says so. He may allow the storm to rage around you but it's to teach you to trust in Him. He wants to walk on the water with you. But what's your focus, are you looking to Him, or do you only look to Him in times of need and then let go of His hand?

Storms strengthen us, they allow us to look back and see what we have come through and that we are still going, looking up and ahead. As we walk through a storm with Jesus our confidence grows. We begin to dump what others have said, or we remember it just to spur us on.

We start to believe Jesus; we begin to realise indeed we can do all things when Jesus is beside us. We begin to see our real character or true identity. Who God intended us to be.

We will achieve what He wants to achieve through us. He doesn't ridicule us for trying. He picks us up dusts us off and says, "well done we will go again!"

Hebrews 10 v 36

Patient endurance is what you need now, so that you will continue to do God's will. Then you will receive all that He has promised.

Don't just sit in the boat. Jesus says "come" to Peter, not go. He's already waiting on you, but you need to take the first steps. You need to move your feet. All can be achieved when you put your full trust in Jesus. He can do ALL things through you, not just some but all. Pray big and think big.

Even saying Lord save me is a prayer. You don't need fancy words; in fact, he'd prefer not. Just call on His name and ask Him.

Psalm 34 v 8

O taste and see that the Lord is good: blessed is the man that trusteth in Him.

# Chapter 20    Religion

Romans 10 v 9

If you declare with your mouth, Jesus is Lord and believe in your heart that God raised Him from the dead, you will be saved.

To be saved you need to believe in your heart that Jesus is Lord and to declare it with your mouth; And believe that Jesus rose from the grave. You must also repent and allow the Holy Spirit to transform you. You must be transformed into His image, who you were mean't to be.

Nicodemus was a Pharisee and a member of the Jewish ruling council. He knew the law of God inside out and practised it. Following the law and the traditions to the letter. He understood that Jesus was sent by God but couldn't grasp the idea of being born again. He followed the law and taught it. He loved God and knew Jesus was from Him but didn't recognise Him as the Son of God, the promised Messiah.

John 3 v 5-7

Jesus answered very truly I tell you; no one can enter the Kingdom of God unless they are born of water and the Spirit. Flesh gives birth to flesh, but the Spirit gives birth to Spirit. You should not be surprised at my saying you must be born again.

It is not enough just to go to church, listen to the message, agree with it, leave and live in the world. When you accept Jesus, you must be born again. When you ask and truly repent you will be born again. Being born again does not mean turning 'good living'. It means choosing to live for Jesus, deciding to be led by the Holy Spirit, listening to His promptings and trying not to intentionally sin.

We say the 'sinners' prayer' Asking to be saved and the Lord saves us. A simple prayer acknowledging that Jesus is the son of God, we are sinners, and we ask Him to save us. We then live under the Holy Spirit covered in the blood of Jesus, so that our God sees His son in us. Many people turn away from religion because they believe that the religious look down on them, they condemn them, and they don't welcome them unless they are well dressed. Also believing that they need to follow the ways of that religion, denomination or church.

Galatians 1 v 10

For am I now seeking the approval of man, or of God? Or am I trying to please man? If I were still trying to please man, I would not be a servant of Christ.

People can make up a false identity, not just from what they think, and others say but in who they choose to let others think they are. They concoct an image of who they want others to think they are.

A depressed person May portray themselves as fun, bubbly, the life and soul of the party; all the while inside feeling lonely and broken. They have anger, anguish, sadness, rejection and so many more negative emotions. For example, somebody who was bullied may reject themselves, embarrassed at what they didn't do.

Have you ever been somewhere and felt totally alone? Have you ever felt like a fraud, an impostor? Have you ever thought that if they knew who you really were they would hurt you and reject you? Then we pretend more and more and get caught in the cycle, never really able to be our true self.

The more we pretend we are someone else the harder it is to be truly ourselves. This leads to frustration at yourself and with others for not letting you be down, or sad, expecting you to be happy and upbeat. You will end up with annoying yourself and others, having to maintain the image. Sometimes the real person gets lost, and it is difficult to remember who we really are.

The cycle is hard to beat because if you revert to yourself what if others don't like you? An image is hard to maintain. It's an image, a photograph, a veneer. it's only a snapshot a fleeting moment. We all pose for photos to look our best. Have you ever noticed that natural photographs always look better?

We all want to look our best but it's for other people usually. Jesus knows every part of us, He sees under the false face. He sees our identity not our image. In church a lot of people portray an image, who they think they should be so as to be accepted by others. We believe that if we dress well, speak well, act well then others will see us as good Christians.

That's not what God wants. In the garden He knew were Adam and Eve where, but He wanted them to speak up to say where they were. He made them and knew them. The same with us, we can hide who we are and pretend, covering up our flaws and blemishes, but God still sees them.

God made us in His image to be in a relationship with Him. Not a fake pretend relationship religion is not what God wants, He wants a church, His people unified in one mind to please Him through His Son Jesus.

Even the depressed person has a sense of relief when they can just be themselves. When they take to their bed, unable to open the curtains, hiding from the world lost in their thoughts but preferable to pretending to be someone or something else.

Depression can and will be used by satan to attack. All he needs is a foothold, a doubt, a recurring thought whispered into the ear. He uses the same tactics to control a person's mind. He gives them false beliefs and whispers to them that they should be ashamed, they are not good enough or they haven't done enough.

Psalm 9 v 9

The Lord is a refuge for the oppressed, a stronghold in times of trouble.

The Lord helps the oppressed those being crushed by others, by their own thoughts and by the whispers of satan. He wants to free us all from oppression. When you see your identity in Him you will understand that you are His child, adopted into His family, an heir and joint heir when you accept Jesus.

If you could see how much He, the creator of the heavens and the earth loves you; He gave His Son to die for you and He stands with His arms open waiting to welcome you home.

Home on earth is in who He says you are. We try to bend for others to see and mould ourselves into a perceived identity. But who could possibly mould God? We couldn't mould Him, we couldn't and shouldn't try. We can't even quantify God; we couldn't even possibly begin to think or understand all that He is. He moulds us. He is the Potter, and we are the clay and if we allow Him, He will make something beautiful and amazing from all our brokenness.

In counselling we use a term called self-actualization. This is the aim of counselling, to help get a person to realise and achieve their full potential, their true self. But this is only part of who they can be. It's all self, it's internal about our needs and our own ambitions. If we could take that self-actualised person and hand them over to God and we could watch as He transforms them further, to a person free from fear, worry, anxiety, depression, free and living a joyful life.

In God we can be who He planned us to be, back to that little pristine snowball inside snowman. Perfect in its individuality. Made and created, moulded and shaped, washed white, pristine and sparkling in Christ.

When a painter paints a picture, and someone comes along and says it would be better if only ....... and they apply more paint, more brush strokes, and others apply what they think. Finally, the original is so hidden and completely unrecognisable from the painter's vision. Under the layers off additional paint lies the original and if the painter removes the paint and strips it back, yes some won't like it, but the painter will see his original masterpiece, restored and redeemed from others' opinions.

The original you, may be hidden but you're in the knowledge that the Artist made it and it's exactly how He intended it to be. When we come back to our Lord, and we strive to please only Him we will care less about what others say or think. Others paint won't stick, because we won't need it when the Artist approves.

Our Lord knows our identity, He knows His original, what we are meant to be. Imagine a life not worrying about what others think of us, what others see when they look at us. If we are saved, they will see Jesus in us, a change that can't go unnoticed. A confidence, not in our ability but in His. The Lord came to save us not condemn us. He alone can bind a broken heart. He heals the mind; He is the Lord and only He is able.

Psalm 27 v 1

The Lord is my light and my salvation; whom shall I fear? The Lord is the strength of my life; of whom shall I be afraid?

The Lord is light, in Him the darkness of depression is broken. Jesus is love. He loves the oppressed, those that the religious push away. Jesus was crucified by the religious, religion is not of Him. He loves all and welcomes all. He sees the heart beneath the image. He sees your identity that's waiting to be accepted by you. Asking you to set down the heaviness and accept His path for your life. To allow Him to move in you and to change and transform you into what He planned you to be. His creation, His masterpiece; Being your true self, not having to hide or be ashamed. Not having to pretend and not having to try to impress Him or others. You cannot be more loved or less loved by Him, He just loves you and that will never change.

73

Chapter 21     Whose armour are you wearing?

1 Samuel 17 v 38-39

Then Saul dressed David in his garments and put a bronze helmet on his head and put a coat of mail on him. Then David fastened his sword over his armour and tried to walk, (but he could not) Because he was not used to them. And David said to Saul, "I cannot with these, because I am not used to them" So David took them off.

Saul as king didn't go into battle against Goliath, he was afraid, as was the rest of Israel. David's three older brothers were also there and not one had come out to go against Goliath.

David had been anointed as king in front of all his brothers, when he was still a young teenager. David hadn't even been invited to the sacrifice and the feast that Samuel had arranged to anoint the next king at. He wasn't even regarded by his father. His brothers all looked the part and had good qualities, I'm sure. David was just happy to tend his father sheep. Even though Jesse, the Bethlemite, had servants, he put his son out in the field with the sheep.

After he was anointed, he went back to the sheep. He knew who the Lord said he was. He was the next king. In humility he went back to the field. He sang and was writing songs, ready to learn and do as God thought good but ready to look after the sheep also.

On the day he went to deliver his brothers cheese and bread to the battle, he went bringing sandwiches. He knew his identity in the Lord, he heard the bully Goliath and thought 'I wouldn't think so, you've crossed the line Goliath'.

His brother accused David of evil, saying he was just there to watch the battle.

1 Samuel 17 v 29

But David said "what have I done now? Was it not just a question"

Saul didn't want to go out against Goliath, but he gave David his armour. Dressing him up in what he should have been wearing but lacking the bravery to do it himself. David put it on, and it was too big and too heavy, he couldn't move let alone fight. But David knew that he was the new king at some point and knew that the Lord was with him.

The Lord didn't or doesn't make empty promises. David understood that God saw his potential, He saw who he was, his heart. David fearlessly defended his father's sheep. A humble young man and an obedient young man, not full of pride.

David was not having anyone making fun of his God. He told Saul no thanks and he stuck to his training what he was good at. He knew how to use a slingshot; he knew his strengths. He knew who empowered him. He knew who he was in the Lord. He knew that if the Lord said he was a king, then a king he was.

David had his own armour, and armour that fitted perfectly, an armour that wasn't heavy, and armour that gave protection and strength. His armour was the Lord God of Israel. He listened to who God said his identity was. Saul put his ambitions onto David. He asked David to put on what he said would help he gave David instructions to do this and that. David didn't listen. People will project what they don't have the nerve to do or what they wish they had done onto others. And when that person puts on someone else's hopes ambitions or criticisms it just doesn't fit.

Someone else's plans, opinions of you, never fit perfectly. It is always heavy and burdensome. Only when we dump that baggage and go on our own, with what we want or feel, do we feel lighter, better and more comfortable. It is just easy. When a young person lives as they see themselves, through their eyes not others, they are no longer weird but are unique. We are all unique when we get back to who we were designed to be. Not knowing ourselves is difficult, we can't discern our likes, dislikes our goals and plans. When we realise these things and know our talents life improves.

David knew how to sling a stone, but the Lord put the direction and the power into it. The Lord implanted the stone in Goliaths head. He made the natural into supernatural. The ordinary anointed teenager into a king, the Lord trained him. He put him through the tests and trials, killing the bear and the lion.

What can the Lord do with your teaching, your pas? The training you have received from Him. Will you place it in His hands and sing and be joyful, waiting on the Lord to use it for His glory?

1 Samuel 17 v 47

And that this entire assembly may know that the Lord does not save with the sword or with this spear; For the battle is the Lords and He will hand you over to us.

This is part of what David said to Goliath. He knew whose armour he needed. The battle is always the Lords, He never ever loses, but we have to decide whose armour we are going to wear; what feels comfortable. What fits. What are our strengths and weaknesses and what can God do with all that we have to offer. Just look at David, the runt of the litter. The Lord didn't want his strength, He wanted his heart and his obedience.

1 Samuel 17 v 29

But David said, "what have I done now? Was it not just a question"

Eliab was the eldest brother of David. He accused him of just wanting to watch the battle. We are told that all of Jesse's sons were brought before Samuel to see which the Lord wanted for the next king. Each son had his own view of who he was. Each thinking he will pick me, maybe some saying please don't pick me!

The strong, the tall, the handsome, the anxious, the incapable all watched as each was rejected as the new king. The Lord made each of them but each one's heart was not what the Lord needed. Then Samuel asked, "have you anymore?" Jessie replied that the youngest was out with the sheep. I bet his brothers were saying, no way not the runt! But the Lord knew exactly who He had chosen and made just for that purpose. Each brother would have had different feelings about David being anointed.

David saying, "what have I done now?" Would tell me that life wasn't easy for David. To reply like that would indicate that he was used to being accused by his brothers. It was that for goodness sake! moment. I wonder were his brothers jealous. Three of them went to fight with the King, King Saul. Maybe thinking Samuel was wrong and positioning themselves close to Saul.

How often do our siblings, and our family's opinions and treatments influence who we think we are. When they tell us we can't that we are not able. That's not what we are good at. Everyone has an opinion of each other, judging and criticising.

I wonder what David's mum thought, like most mums did she adore her youngest son. Her little underdog. Anointed to be king. It seems to me that the only one in the family who truly knew who he was, and his ability, was David. Did he ever remind them who he was or did he just let them 'rattle on'. Confident and self-assured in his true identity. Confident in who the Lord said he was in Him, and what His will for his life was to be.

David saw the hand of God on him, he was filled with the Holy Spirit when Samuel anointed him. But still he was bullied by his siblings. What did he learn, did he learn to dislike bullies, did he understand what was wrong with his brothers, was he sympathetic or did he just look up?

It's the same with us all. We can get so far holding onto past hurts, criticisms, taunts and failures. We can even let that shape and mould our image, who others see and who we see. Image is a snapshot, a small glimpse; It can be edited and taken out of context, it can be destroyed.

Identity is different. Identity is that little snowball inside of a snowman, white, pure and pristine. Still in there, but maybe hidden away for fear of rejection. Covered and protected by layers. When we accept Jesus and the Holy Spirit removes the layers of armour, the sticky labels attached to us; we are brought back to who God designed us to be.

We were made in God's image. We were created to be like Him. With His ways, the Lord created us to commune with us.

Our true identity is honest and truthful. We don't have to hide who we are in shame, feeling we are not enough. The Lord tells us in Ephesians 6 v 11 to put on His full armour. He protects us, He loves us, and He knows us warts and all. David, throughout all, saw the Lords careful hand. He trusted Him and believed Him. He was not afraid to swim upstream, against the crowd. When he was crowned king, his brothers fought for him in his armies. They finally saw who the Lord said he was.

Look always to who the Lord knows you are. Seek His will. Accept Him as your Saviour and put down all that has gone before and be a new creation in Him. Let Him tell you your identity, what you can achieve with Him working in and through you.

His armour fits you perfectly, it is impenetrable so light. Only your heart and soul knows that you are even wearing it. But God knows that He has crafted it just for you. Take off others armour and wear His.

## Chapter 22    The truth

John 8 v 32

And you will know the truth and the truth will set you free.

In the world, the dictionary meaning of truth means the body of real things true events and facts; the state of being the case; truth in the Bible is that which is consistent with the mind, will, character, glory and being of God. In Aramaic it means equity evenly weighed or reality.

One of the 10 commandments given to Moses on Mount Sinai is, you shall not testify falsely (that is, lie, withhold, or manipulate the truth) against your neighbour (any person).

Lies are the weapon of the enemy, he tells half-truths and lies. He whispers in your ear telling you, you can't do that, you're unlovable, inadequate, inferior, incapable. 'In' As a prefix can mean 'not' in other words not adequate not capable. 'Un' as a prefix also means not, not lovable, not worthy, not acceptable. All words that when used mean that we have fallen short.

We can apply these words to ourselves and always live a life that is not good enough, changing our behaviour to fit. Not trying, people pleasing (basing who we are on our ability to make others happy), becoming shy, introvert. Being humble in human terms, putting ourselves down, inside feeling hurt, angry and resentful.

These words are usually applied because of our experiences. Feeling ignored at home parents who are fighting and arguing a lot, siblings who demand all the attention, suicides of friends or family, bullying also can make us feel as if the bully is correct and that we must change our personality because of the bullying.

An excluded child may feel as if they don't belong, and no one likes them. Their trust will be damaged and may be ruined. Trust is a reliance and belief that something or someone is honest and real. To trust we must get to know try and test. Many young people and adults find it hard to trust their own feelings, other people and things that they see. The enemy if he can ruin trust with lies and half-truths can try to separate us and keep us from the truth of God.

When we listen to lies told to us by our parents they can stick. A parent who projects all that they have failed at onto a child or young person. If the parent believes the lies that they themselves have been told, how can they love a child openly and build them up. How can a parent help a child to their full potential if they have lived at defeated life.

We are all a product off our parents or are main caregiver. If we are nurtured, usually we can live a life more confidently and have more trust in our abilities and what we can do and achieve.

Jesus is the Son of God. He has and is the best parent our Abba, Hebrew for daddy.

John 5 v 19

Jesus replied, "truly I tell you, the Son is not able to do anything on His own, but only what He sees the Father doing. For whatever the Father does, the Son likewise does these things"

Jesus could only do what His Father God did. He was a perfect reflection of God in all His ways. His full character, His grace, His mercy and most of all His love for all. Yet God loved you so much He sent His perfect sinless Son to die for our sins. Jesus loved His Father and us so much that in obedience He gave up His life, so that through our belief in Him, we could be saved and reconciled to the Father, God.

Who do you look to? Who do you follow? Who is your example? If your role model is anxious and you see their reactions to certain situations the truth is that you will probably be anxious also.

Do you remember doing exams and thinking "I've done OK" until you come out and your friend says, "what did you put for this question?" If you put something different you will question what you have written, you may think that their answer is the truth. Only knowing what's correct when it has been marked. But the anxiety of not knowing the truth is horrible.

Over COVID and lock down there were a lot of lies and deceptions peddled. A lot of half-truths. Yes, people died, but the media caused so much distress and anxiety to so many people; Driving people to isolate and stay indoors. Please don't misunderstand me I believe Covid is and was real, as I lost family members, but there were so many lies told.

Truth can be bent to set another agenda, to help them achieve the outcome they want. Even the smallest lie can do a lot of damage. Have you ever say, bent the truth or told a white lie? All are still lies. A lie must be maintained to make it believable and for the teller to stay credible.

A lie of any size can be used by the devil as a means of achieving a foothold. He can taunt you with it, and it can be used to unsettle you, to attack you. We don't fear the lie, but it is its consequences on us and on others. Those we lie to or those we lie about

Consider for example, a young man accused of rape by a disgruntled girlfriend. Mud sticks and some would rather believe a lie as it seems to them more interesting. A person accused of inappropriate behaviours or words. Lies usually do not have evidence. It's one person's word against another's, and the crowd is usually divided. Lies stick and so many lives can be changed and damaged because of these lies.

The person who is lied about may become over vigilant, never able to fully trust or relax. The doubt and the mistrust placed in their minds will stop trust, like satan in the garden of Eden putting doubt in the minds of Adam and Eve. He always uses the same tactics.

As it is one person's word against the other, so too with the Lord, we have His word, the Bible, the word of God. The word that makes the world spin, that created all. Versus the word of the world and the enemy. Who do you listen to? What is your truth? One way leads to salvation and the other way to destruction.


Ephesians 4 v 25

Therefore, each of you must put off falsehood and speak truthfully to your neighbour, for we are all members of one body.

Throughout the Bible we are warned against telling lies. Let me put it this way, what is better, to tell the truth or to tell lies? Each one saved or unsaved knows the difference between lies and truth. lies can damage and ruin all involved. Truth may sometimes be painful, but it is true and so is fact. If the Bible was not of God, then why is it full of truth, telling you how to live a fulfilled happy life.

It warns against lies and the damage and destruction it can inflict. The devil is the prince of lies. It's all he knows how to do and that leads to destruction and to sin and eventually death. Nothing good can come from lies, because there is no good in the enemy. It goes against his character so therefore he can only lie, steal, deceive and destroy.

Jesus stood quietly as He was falsely accused, they brought false witnesses telling lies about Him, but nothing was able to be proved as it was false. There was no evidence, remember lies have no evidence. Truth has evidence to back the claims, as they are true. Jesus healed so many who were transformed, there was a great body of evidence.

Jesus was truth and still is truth. Many people could testify and still do testify and tell what He did and is still doing for them. His claims can be backed up and proved. He is who He says He is.

Jesus performed so many miracles on earth. He healed diseases, gave sight to the blind, hearing to the deaf, and cast out demons. Even the demons knew the truth even though they couldn't follow it. They knew Jesus was the Son of God, the Messiah. They fell before Him and cried out to Him, for mercy, that He would not destroy them. He did not lift his hand against the legions of demons but granted what they asked for, mercy, and drove them into the herd of pigs. The pigs fell off the cliffs and the demons were destroyed.

Jesus grants mercy to all who ask Him. Jesus is the truth; all His ways are truth.

Proverbs 12 v 17

An honest witness tells the truth, but a false witness tells lies.

Truth means honesty, lies are false by definition. You may not like some of the things says in the Bible and choose not to accept Jesus because of it, and that is your choice, but the truth is that Jesus loves you. The word of God is the way to salvation, redemption and eternal life; a happy, truthful, abundant life.

Some of the Bible is difficult for us to apply, but even so it is still the truth. The Lord Jesus through the power of the Holy Spirit helps us. He is the truth and the only way to God, and therefore heaven. So many people believe the lies of the enemy, that if they are a good person, or someone prays for them to go to heaven, or pays money then they will get to heaven.

The so-called 'Rainbow Bridge'? This isn't in the Bible, so this also isn't the way to heaven. Only faith in Jesus as the Lord and Saviour can save you. He's the only way and He wants none to be lost. Salvation is available for you now, just as you are, not the cleaned up sober version, but now. Don't let the lies of Satan separate you from who God says you are in Him. trust in who He says He is and look for the evidence. Ask Him and He will save you, He turns none away, who truly believe in Him.

Chapter 23    Relationships

1 Thessalonians 5 v 11

Encourage one another and build each other up, just as in fact you are doing.

We are all in relationships, it's what teaches us and shows us how to live and interac with others. Our first relationship is with our mother and father or whoever is our main caregiver. Increasingly family means so many different things. It can be mum and dad and children, mum and children, dad and children, only child, multiple kids, same sex parents and different parents from our siblings.

The big thing is how we experience these relationships. Are they encouraging, nurturing and loving? Or are they destructive broken and unsafe maybe? All are different but we all need relationships, we need company we crave acceptance and love. We all want to feel safe and trust those around us, and also feel trusted.

All children need a 'secure base', one constant in their life, the one they go to, the unchanging, always there for them, person. Ideally this would be a parent, but it could be sibling, a grandparent, an aunt or anyone who makes the person feel loved and secure.

A child born into a 'Rocky' relationship, watching and hearing arguments, will become a good reader of people and atmospheres. We may look at people with this quality and think it admirable, but we don't maybe understand the reason they have learned that skill.

Usually in a marriage break up the 'secure base', the constant will receive all the anger and bad behaviour; whilst the one who left will be treated well by the child or young person. I have asked numerous young people, and all give the same answer; they say tha they know that they can be angry with that person because they also realise, they won't leave so they trust them more. So, if you are in that position talk to them, as you are doing a great job.

It's like when you drop your child off at school or nursery, if the child walks in and waves it's usually because they are confident that you will be back for them. A child crying and refusing to leave a parent may mean that that child is feeling insecure in that relationship. It doesn't mean that they love you as a parent more than the other children that go on in to school love their parents. They just have worries in their minds.

A child who doesn't express their anger usually becomes what's called passive aggressive. This is like when someone says something to you smiling but you feel you've just been attacked, but you can't prove it. It's the angry person who was always punished or ridiculed for speaking their mind. They find other ways to express how they feel in a more non-threatening way.

This is called a defence mechanism, it keeps the person from being direct, able to deny if the response is wrong or too aggressive or challenging. This can be used in controlling, manipulative or abusive relationships. When we go into a relationship, we don know the full story of the other person. For example, imagine a young man who has been treated with anger and aggression, made to feel as if he was unworthy, being in a relationship with a girl who watched an abusive parent, he put her down and maybe hit he or controlled her.

The product could be a woman who controls with put downs and a partner who retaliates with more veiled comments, this can apply to either men or women. We all learn from our examples. Be aware that we all argue as parents, or partners but it's how we deal with it. Some people would say that they don't argue in front of their children as if that's a great thing, and in a way it is. As long as the children cannot hear from another room. It's the atmosphere, the slightly raised tone of voice, the ignoring each other, children watch and know the signs.

Then this becomes and translates into the child, he may want to please and keep the peace, they don't say how they feel, they internalise things and try to be good. If this continues into adulthood, this can lead to a 'people pleaser'. What I mean by that is someone who goes over and above trying to make others feel good, happy to try and make themselves feel liked. They base how they feel on their ability to make others happy. their self-esteem being directly linked to their experience of others. They will never be happy as they will never be liked or able to please everyone.

They overthink always replaying conversations. Trying to gauge if they are liked. They always look to the external things and their effect on them. They don't consider do they like others. Always considering themselves annoying or the cause of problems. Don't get me wrong even people who have grown up in what we would call a good home can still have bad experiences through school, friendship, deaths and other influences.

1 Peter 4 v 8

Above all, love each other deeply because love covers over a multitude of sins.

This is what matters most, love. Love makes a child feel happier and more secure no matter what the circumstances and being loved not just by one person. To feel loved and accepted by a few or lots makes a person feel safe, secure, lovable and more confident and ready to live life, knowing that they have loved ones to support them.

God is love; His Son Jesus loved us so much that He died to save us. Even when Jesus rose from the dead, alive again He went back to His Father in heaven. He learned from His Father and watched what He did. When we accept Jesus, we are adopted into God's family, an heir and a joint heir with Jesus.

Jesus then becomes our 'secure base', the one we can rely on. Jesus never changes. He doesn't wait to punish us, as many think, but He stands waiting to welcome us and to love us. He doesn't want us to have religion, He simply wants us to have faith and to accept His free gift of salvation.

Imagine being in a relationship and your partner saying I love you if only you behave in a certain way, dress a certain way, drive a certain car, share the same opinions and treat me in a certain way, but they can treat you however they please? Some people are in these relationships, and then they wonder why they feel so unhappy, burdened never good enough and on the edge.

That's not a relationship; yes, we all need to tweak things about each other usually, merely bad habits, but if we must change who we are completely into whom someone believes they will be happier with, that's not my idea of love. People lose themselves in a relationship like this and it's not healthy.

In a healthy relationship we can be fully ourselves and because we love each other we will do our best to please that other person but not at the expense of ourselves. If you love someone deeply you won't want that person change who they are.

When we come to Jesus, He already knows us inside out, He doesn't want to change who we are, just our behaviour if it is destructive to us and others. The Lord knows our motives and can judge if we're doing harm by how we behave.

Romans 15 v 7

You will bring God glory when you accept and welcome one another as partners, just as the Anointed One (Jesus) has fully accepted you and receives you as His partner.

We are to welcome and love each other as Jesus has loved and welcomed us. Jesus doesn't weigh us down with unreasonable requests. He encourages us, He loves us, He died for us, He protects us, He is a rock we can stand on, immoveable and unshakeable. He doesn't change, and His character is always the same. He doesn't have a bad day. Even when He was crucified, He asked His Father to forgive them.

Jesus wants to illuminate our path and place our feet on His path. He never leaves or forsakes us. He is always a constant. Even at your ugliest He sees your beauty, even at your weakest He sees your strength. When you are worried, He comforts you and He fights for you.

He only wants the best for you and will never let you down. He will always be just and faithful to you. He won't abandon you or reject you. He will go through trials with you and asks only that you talk to Him, read His word and trust and believe in Him.

Romans 5 v 8

But God demonstrates His own love for us in this; while we were still sinners, Christ died for us.

God loves us even before we are the cleaned-up version. He loves us just as we are. He wants to show us who we are in Him; our identity as He the creator of all made us. He loves all our wee ways. He accepts us just as we are, and we don't even understand how much He loves us. When we realise this, we will want to change, not to try and earn salvation, it's a free gift, but we change because we will love Him, because He loved us, and He died for us.

It's difficult to believe but easy to receive. How could anyone let alone God love us as we are, with all our flaws, the things that we have said, done and thought. But He does He just loves us all and wants us all to believe that Jesus is the Son of God and He died for us. So that all our past sins, present sins and future sins could be paid for with His sacrifice and the blood He spilled for us.

It's mind blowing yet its requirements are simple because it is available to all. It's not just for the clever, the rich, the respectable. It's for the sinner, the broken, the one who's at rock bottom. Abused, angry, addicted, defeated, all types of people. He calls all and wants to save all who will accept Him and trust in Him. He wants us to be genuine to come before Him as we are, not pretending knowing we couldn't possibly deserve it. He tells us He came to seek and save the lost. If you are lost and broken you are exactly who He came for, come as you are and let Him tell you who you were made to be. Let Him transform you.

# Chapter 24    Blame

Proverbs 28 v 13

He who covers his sins will not prosper. But whoever confesses and forsakes them will have mercy.

Have you ever done something that you knew was wrong and you didn't confess to anyone or try to put it right? Most people do have something. It can either niggle at you and gently nudge you, or it can feel huge and eat away at you in huge chunks. All these hidden things will change who you are, and how you are to varying degrees. All hidden sin, even one we think we have buried, can resurface at the most unexpected times. They can be brought up by 'triggers'. The same situation or similar, seeing it in someone else or the feelings we have around it can all bring up memories, either good or bad.

Guilt is the feeling that we haven't done enough, or we are guilty of doing something. It can be fixed, apologised for, confessed or even the blame shifted to someone else. Shifting blame only allows temporary relief. There is no worse feeling, in my opinion than being falsely accused and all believing it; the whispers and people distancing themselves, not wanting to be associated with you. Either through believing or fear that they too would be accused.

Jesus was blamed, accused and judged. Mocked, beaten, scorned, spat on, kicked, whipped and crucified. He was blameless. He took on His body all our sin. He took the blame for us all and took the penalty for it. His disciples scattered; they disowned Him. They went back to their old jobs and hid away in fear that they too would suffer the same death.

They scattered even as He was arrested. Only John was at the foot of the cross with Mary. He was a young man, courageous, and he went to the foot of the cross with love.  At the foot of the cross was Mary Magdalene, Jesus' mother Mary, Mary of Cleopas and Salome, Jesus' mother Mary's sister.

The people walked by taunting Him and looking at Him with hate and self-righteousness. The two men on either side of Him, each also on a cross, both sinners. One mocked Him as well; Telling Jesus to save Himself and them. He said it sarcastically and with a hardened heart. The second man told the first to shut up and leave Him alone.

He knew he deserved his punishment, and he acknowledged that Jesus didn't deserve this death. He asked Jesus to remember him when He got to His kingdom. He knew who Jesus was and that He was going to His Kingdom, and by asking Him to remember him he had asked Jesus to save him.

Jesus told him that today he would be in paradise with Him. He was genuine in his acknowledgment and his repentance. Jesus suffered beside him and died the same death. One sinner was at peace, the other going to damnation but both had the same opportunity to repent and ask for forgiveness. Jesus doesn't force us.

James 1 v 13

let no one say when he is tempted, "I am tempted by God"; for God cannot be tempted by evil, nor does He Himself tempt anyone.

God does not make us sin, He may allow things to happen, as a means of teaching but there is no darkness in God. Remember learning for example, how to ride a bike? you fall off and hurt yourself, maybe even breaking an arm, but eventually you learn and realise how to ride, and you can then ride your bike safely and enjoy it. This is what it is like with trials, it may be hard, but we learn in them about us, and others and if we seek Him, about God.

If we carry about guilt, it's hard to forget about and set to one side, the best we can do is, maybe, to tell someone. Guilt is usually, not just what we have or have not done, it snowballs into consequences, judgement, fear and all that is negative. We don't look at that one thing, we think about what others will say and think about us. A relatively small thing can become a mountain. Hard to get around or forget about.

Being accused wrongly, guilt and shame are the age-old tactics of the devil, it's all he knows. He couldn't hurt Adam and Eve physically, but he attacks the mind. He tries through lies and our insecurities and experiences to control our thoughts, trying to get us to sin, hurt ourselves or others.

Proverbs 23 v 7

For as he thinks in his heart, so is he...

If you think you are guilty, wrong, insecure or shameful then you will behave accordingly. Your behaviour will change and how you see yourself will change. Addictions may serve a purpose, taking your mind also thoughts and memories; Making you take a break from believing all the add on thoughts and views you have about yourself.

Remember that you were made in God's image, that's who you are. This is how sin entered the world, when satan took a hold of Eve's mind and planted thoughts that shouldn't have been there. But planting a thought is so easy and can be very destructive. It can be through a word or an action of someone else and our imagination will run riot.

We were not meant to be like this, guilt and shame robs us of our peace. The peace that allows us to be joyful in the Lord. The accused person, accused of lying, crimes, of doing things we didn't do all wreck our peace. It can ruin trust and our faith in others.

Trust, faith and belief are all qualities we need to follow Christ. If the enemy does a good enough job, he can completely tie someone up in knots obscuring the truth. They may get so sceptical, and see all as untrustworthy, and they may become blinded by the work of the enemy.

Matthew 11 v 28-30

Come to Me, all you who are weary and burdened, and I will give you rest. Take My yoke upon you and learn from Me, for I am gentle and humble in heart, and you will find rest for your souls. For My yoke is easy and My burden is light.

The Lord loves us all and He knows when you have been falsely accused and the truth will always come out. The Lord wants us all to have peace of mind. He wants us to be at rest mentally, not being taunted, condemned and beaten down. The child who waits to be beaten will learn to tell lies. The child of accused of things will either feel the injustice or may decide "Well I'm being accused so I may as well do it!"

Please see that all the enemies' tactics, lies, that are placed in our minds cause us to stray further from our identity. We were designed and made to be in fellowship with a Holy God. Adam and Eve, as sinless were able to walk with God in the garden each day, before the sin came. Adam and Eve hid from God, and He spoke to them. He made them clothes and because of the sin, they couldn't live forever.

We also are estranged from God because of our sin. The only way we can be reinstated to our true identity is through Jesus. When we realise our need of a Saviour; when we believe that He is the Son of God and that He died for our sins and we ask Him to save us and we repent, leading or trying and persevering, to lead a new life in faith and trust and belief in Him.

The faith, trust and belief that the enemy tries to keep from us and to steal who we are. If he can pollute our minds and try to steal the truth from us, we will never know our true identity, potential and enjoy the easy yoke and the light burden that the Lord gives us. We were not meant to have poor mental health, depression and other various psychological conditions that cause harm. We were created to have joy, peace, gentleness, no malice, no envy, no hatred and no anger. We were to live happy, peaceful purposeful lives. Our lives were to reflect the glory of God, as His creations His children.

Even Christians can have poor mental health when we listen to the enemy, even those in church, knowingly and unknowingly being used to knock us. To ruin our confidence, steal our peace and accuse us, all from a whisper of the enemy.

Again, the same tactics as he always uses, with the same results until we realise what he's up to. These tactics can cross generations and give varying degrees of success. What I mean is if he can destroy a child or a parent the consequences can affect others too, then guilt, blame and shame can continue to work for him.

Only when we set down all before our Lord and Saviour, asking Him to cover our ears and allow us to believe His word, His truth. When we trust in Him and what He can do and who He is and says we are in Him, and when we continue with Him in faith; Then the enemy will flee, and we will grow into who we are in Him. We will reflect Him, and our identity is and will be as He tells us. We will believe who He says He is.

# Chapter 25    Identity

1 John 3 v 2

Dear friends, now we are children of God, and what we will be has not yet been made known. But we know that when Christ appears, we shall be like Him, or we shall see Him as He is.

You are God's creation, created in His image. Created for a purpose. People without hope usually will say "what's the point?", "What am I here for?" No one can answer that except the Lord, He made each of us different and uniquely. Each one of us has qualities and skills that He has given us. We all have talents.

Let me ask you do you live with an image or an identity? An image by definition is just that, a photograph. It's a veneer, shiny, polished up and posed for. A snapshot of the good stuff. What we present to the world, like social media, we put the highlights up.

People see the smiles and the location and the fun. They don't see the underlying true story. You could be really living your best life with not a care in the world, but that is not usually the case for so many. Most want to project an image of a perfect life. They want to portray what they would like others to think they are like, or their life is like.

An image is very fragile it can be easily destroyed, and it can be manipulated to fit. Sometimes an image has to be maintained and can be used to step all over someone else. If someone challenges an image because they can see through it, this can be hurtful for all parties.

An image can be constructed as a way of keeping a person safe. Almost like an armour protecting the fragile interior from attack or exposure. As some people would say "if they dislike who I'm pretending to be at least the real me is still safe and they can't hurt it", it is or can be something that they learn to do to protect themselves.

Matthew 6 v 2-3

Whenever you give to the poor, don't blow your trumpet as the hypocrites do in the synagogues and in the streets so that they may get praise from people. I assure you, that's the only reward they'll get. But when you give to the poor don't let your left hand know what your right hand is doing.

We are to do all we do discreetly and if possible, in secret. If we do it openly then we are doing it to impress man, and not God. A lot of people, especially on social media love to be portrayed as caring and sharing, loving and giving. If as Christians we do this for man's approval, we sin. We are to give as an honour to our Father in Heaven. We are always to look to glorify Him. To do all in His name giving Him praise.

We must remember the Lord knows our identity. He sees always under the veneer, the image. the Lord knows the motives of the heart. The Lord sees who it is we want to impress, who we hold in higher regard than Him. As humans of course we all love a pat on the back from those we love, know and our peers. Remember as a child doing well and getting praise for your achievements?

Doing well allowed us to feel good about ourselves. To feel love and appreciation. We all love a bit of praise; it gives us confidence and belief in what we can do. Encouragement allows us to move forward and strive for more. In churches, sometimes people have more of an image than an identity and they try to uphold the image more than to be transformed into who God says we are in His image.

The happy family who are secretly on the brink of divorce, with the image of a perfect family. Pretending all is good and not able to show the truth for fear of what others may think of them and their image. Not wanting others to see the problem; even though as a Church of believers we are to share each other's burdens.

The Lord sees and hears all, He hears the arguments, the anxiety, maybe the violence and the unfaithfulness; The addictions in whatever form they take. But always remember the Lord knows the full story. He sees each heart and hurts from the beginning. He sees the consequences and the results of positive and negative words. An image can be changed by a simple caption, or a narrative, it can be distorted. Some people turn others into idols wanting to be like them, but believing the hype, that image.

I was once told that I was just like my father, and I was so pleased and happy about that. My dad wouldn't have wanted that even though he loved me. My dad, Jerry, would want me to be in the image of my Heavenly Father. To strive for my identity in Christ.

When we know our identity, who we are as people and are not afraid to let others see this, to not try and hide and to say what we think without fear we will be more comfortable with what we say and think. We will be more able to do as we want, within reason, and without hurting others. To like ourselves warts and all and to appreciate who we are and to not try to show a false image.

When we are genuine and honest with others, they will trust us, they may not like us, but they will admire our ability to speak our mind. In counselling we call this process self-actualization. Stripping away the hurts and the negative influences that would cause pain and discouragement. Self-actualization allows a person to achieve and recognise their full potential.

If an individual can realise their identity, it will make them feel more real, authentic and ultimately a lot happier. They won't need to fear being called out or the image being seen for what it is. Trying to uphold the lie of who they are not.

When Jesus steps in and the person accepts His image that's when the miraculous happens. Even when we are being ourselves, we will never be truly happy, there will always be something missing. We will still search and strive. A better house, a better car, a more exotic holiday, a nicer nose, a tighter face! Whatever it is we go after we will never be fully happy.


Psalm 34 v 4

I saw the Lord, and He answered me and delivered me from all my fears.

Fear makes us strive after the wrong things. Not wanting to be seen as lacking, inferior or not as good as others. The Lord understands this as He has been with us from the beginning and has seen everything and knows everything. A lack of money in the family growing up can make us envy others and all that they have achieved, not allowing us to realise that that person that we envy will envy us for other things.

When we come to Jesus in repentance and He saves us, we are set free from fear. We will be His reflection. We will become like Him. our identity is in Christ. He strips away all, He doesn't leave us comfortless, but He loves us and moves in us as a loving Father. He gently helps us, as on our own we are frail and ultimately weak and only He can strengthen us.

In Jesus we are strong, He who picks us. He, through the work of the Holy Spirit transforms us into His image. The Holy Spirit is always there to illuminate Jesus, to shine light on Him. To put the spotlight on Him who sacrificed Himself out of pure love. To save us now, today just as we are.

Psalm 34 v 8

O taste and see that the Lord is good: blessed is the man that trusteth in Him.

The Lord wants you to see for yourself, to ask Him and to trust Him; not the cleaned-up version but just as you are.

Acts 4 v 12

Neither is there salvation in any other: but there is none other name under Heaven given among man, whereby we must be saved.

Only Jesus and through Him, and calling on His name, asking Him can you be saved. You can't go to Heaven without being saved by Jesus.

Acts 2 v 21

And it shall come to pass, that whosoever shall call on the name of the Lord shall be saved.

Anyone at all can call on the name of Jesus and be saved as we are all equal in His eyes. Jesus is no regarder of people. He knows your heart and all that you have done, all that you are, and He still loves you and calls you, He wants to save you. He wants to show you, your identity in Him. You don't try to fit the Lord into who you think He is. Give Him free reign and let Him show you who you are in Him.

Luke 19 v 10

For the Son of Man has come to seek and save that which was lost.

That's all of us, we were all lost and some still are. Jesus gives us an invitation to eternal life with Him. He wants you to live a happy abundant life, filled with love. He wants you to set down all your preconceptions of who He is and let Him show you who you are, let Him take you on a journey with Him, and discover your identity in Him.

Will you ask Him, and will you accept Him? When we realise that we are all sinners, we all sin every day and He still loves us and waits for us to call on His name. He turns none away. If you are not saved and would like to be you can say this small but massive prayer?

Lord Jesus, I believe that you are the Son of God. I believe you died on the cross for my sin. I believe and I know that I am a Sinner. I ask You to forgive me my sins and to save me. To come into my heart and change me. Thank you, Jesus. Amen.

.

Printed in Great Britain
by Amazon

32237784R00056